Paul Roës

Music, the Mystery and the Reality

English version by Edna Dean McGray

E&M Publishing
6711 East Avenue
Chevy Chase, Maryland ~~20015~~ 20815

ISBN 0-9601832-1-3

Library of Congress Catalog Card Number 78-59815

Printed in the United States of America
Corporate Press, Inc.
2414 Douglas Street, Northeast, Washington, D.C. 20018

This work is lovingly dedicated to the memory of
Marcella Palmer Blanchard

Editor's Preface

La Musique Mystère et Réalité, the fifth and final book of Paul Roës, is particularly important for scholarly pianists, performers and teachers who have already explored fields of technique and esthetics. It incorporates all of the ideas and theories that occupied the author during his lifetime. It was designated by his wife as the one for translation, although there is much yet to be gleaned from earlier small books beginning with *Essai sur la Technique du Piano,* published in 1935, which developed from a series of twelve lectures.

The general character of *La Musique* is at the same time philosophical and practical; esthetical in a unique fashion, yet extremely technical. The principal musicians that Roës studies are Beethoven, Chopin, Liszt and Busoni; he also relates many personal experiences with notable artists of his time; and he is not without humor, despite his serious dedication and his reverence for sound.

All is related to sound: initiation, duration and evanescence; its mysteries; its realities in demanding the utmost from the performer.

There are interesting conclusions concerning some controversial areas in piano technique, such as: seating, high or low; digital dexterity, (is it finger independence, or perhaps finger isolation?); weight, (is it pressure, or using gravity as a natural resource?). The ultimate goal of Roës was always ease of playing; to make the best possible use of the piano as the instrument; to use the body facilities much as a dancer uses the floor for his point of departure.

Among the myriad of benefits to be derived from keeping this volume around for re-reading and studying are: his emphasis on self-teaching as the proper goal for any master to develop with his pupil; "first music, then studies"; "resting the ear" as imperative, in order always to maintain the highest level of acuteness in listening to one's own playing; the importance of a performing artist as not isolating himself from people and the world outside his own musical existence—"All our playing is but the reflection of what we are."

La Musique Mystère et Réalité was for certain the culmination of Roës' life's work as concert pianist, composer, writer and teacher, as the manuscript was unpublished at the time of his death on May 15, 1955. Through efforts of his widow, Mme. E. Roës-Houwink, and friends, publication was realized that same year.

Paul Roës was born in Wageningin, Holland. His first piano lessons were with his mother. At age seventeen he went to Amsterdam for further instruction under Anton Thiery and Julius Röntgen. In 1911

he began his studies with Ferruccio Busoni in Berlin, with whom he maintained a lifelong friendship.

His first recital was in London at Acolian Hall, just before the outbreak of World War I in 1914. Subsequent concert tours included Germany, Austria, Switzerland, France, Holland, England and Italy. Under the management of Baldini and Tremaine of New York City, his first appearance in the United States of America was in December of 1925, with a return engagement in 1927.

His concerts received good reviews. They praise in particular his fine interpretations of Beethoven and Chopin. The reviews also praise his own compositions, which were frequently a part of the programs.

In 1929, the Roës family settled in Paris, where they lived for the rest of Paul's life, and Mme. Roës occupied the same flat until her death on March 29, 1976. Clearly, Roës' inclinations turned more and more to composition, writing and teaching (one wonders if the intervention of two World Wars was an influence in this direction). He did not completely abandon his concert playing; however, the emphasis remained on writing and teaching. To quote Mme. Marie Stuart de Backer, student of Roës in Paris, as well as their friend: "Pupils from all over Europe came to him after 1945, some already very well known, and they did not hesitate to modify their technique according to his principles, finding thereafter ease and relaxation."

Accuracy of presentation in this translation has been my foremost goal, and therefore all my copy was sent to Mme. Stuart for her corrections and suggestions. A time arrived when general consensus determined that a few deletions were absolutely necessary in order not to interrupt the author's train of thought. In March of 1973 I set out for seven days in Paris to meet two women who had become first-name friends through some six years of correspondence, to discuss and obtain approval for the editing. It was truly a memorable experience with two superior people—Mme. E. Roës-Houwink (affectionately referred to by her friends as "Eke," "Ekie," "Kakey") and Mme. Marie Stuart de Backer.

On one of the afternoons in Paris, after high tea with Eke in her flat, just one short block from Balzac's house, business was suddenly the order of the day. The air seemed charged with tension as dialogue in French flew between Eke and Marie, while the former made a microscopic examination of the text. It was obvious that Eke, then in her eighties, held in her memory every word that Paul had written. A witness to this intensity was present—my sister, Roberta Best—who was supposedly quietly reading a book. Later, Roberta and I discovered that we had simultaneously felt the moment of relaxation.

All of a sudden Eke burst out in English, "You are absolutely right. Now, what do you have on your title page? Let me see it." She then

rearranged the title page to her satisfaction, specifying the words "English version by Edna Dean McGray."

The translation follows the text faithfully, with very little editing. Deletions or alterations are mostly in Chapter Two, as described below.

Rudolf M. Breithaupt is introduced in Roës' text as an important figure in the discussion of "great interpreters" and their relation to the technical theorists who preceded Breithaupt. Here I have substituted a reference to Amy Fay's book for a listing of purely names.

A lengthy listing of the violin family tree and all of its descendants from the three schools of violin out of Leopold Auer, Martin Marsick and Otakar Sėvčik was deleted. The important elements remain, i.e.: Roës' respect for "a true confraternity among violinists"; his emphasis on importance of the whole physical attitude, as he illustrates by Marsick's direction to a young student, "Do you feel at ease standing up, does your body rest well on the pelvis? No? . . . you do not feel it? . . . Come back and see me when you have achieved this."

One short passage has been transferred to the appendix. It consists of commendations for a group of musicians who were actively engaged in continuing the precepts of Liszt at the time of Roës' writing, the early 1950's. It remains important, though I felt it was an unnecessary digression in the part of the text where he is developing his thesis.

An excellent scholar called attention to a few details that had no basis of fact. Without doubt Roës' authorities were in error; nevertheless, this resulted in a search for factual information, and, when a detail proved unimportant to the main objective, it was omitted. For example, Siloti's death was confirmed by several sources, including the Library of Congress, as occurring in New York, not in Paris. In just a few instances, "so-and-so" proved not to have studied with "so-and-so." No medical authority sustained Roës' reference to Chopin's fifth finger being evidence of the ailment that caused his death.

The original music examples, containing the author's own markings, are indispensable to the text and these are reproduced with the French publisher's permission. A few obvious errors in notation are corrected by hand.

•

Marcella Palmer Blanchard, who died on December 10, 1967, began this translation, which was just one part of a comprehensive study that we were doing. It was she who made our first contact, through correspondence, with Paul Roës' widow. Marcella was an individual who in her later years overcame crippling disabilities in order to pursue her goal. The example of her unconquerable spirit has bolstered my determination to complete the task.

Subsequently the work became a matter of interpretation, an attempt to "enter the mind of another" through his writings. In this respect it would have remained partly tentative speculation without the aid of one who had close association with the author as student, fellow musician and friend: Marie Stuart de Backer.

In addition, my personal musical inspiration for some twenty years has been Konrad Wolff, who led Marcella and me to the writings of Paul Roës. Without his direction any time it was needed this translation might never have been accomplished.

I am most grateful for Colonel Wendell Blanchard's aid, also that of Marcella and Wendell's daughter Carol Blanchard Gochenour, who helped her mother with the first rough draft. Valuable advice and suggestions came from Donald Garvelmann, and Helen Cooke supplied a final editing. Lastly, I thank many other friends and relatives who have listened to my agonizing.

E.D.M.

Table of Contents

PART II: THE BIRTH OF A METHOD

Table of Illustrations

Preface

This book is addressed not only to musicians, professional and amateur, but also, in great part, to those who find in art, and in music especially, a diversion from their everyday preoccupations.

Part I emphasizes the universal character of art, while summarizing the philosophical theses. We have separated the scientific and historical considerations from the core idea, allowing us to set into relief the predominant thought of this work.

Thus the "Legacy of Liszt" is not at all a biography; it reveals the radiance of Liszt's spirit and his influence on his contemporaries, which spreads even to our times.

The chapters are connected without going into detail or elaborating upon the known facts, any of which would amply support a treatise by itself.

"The Birth of a Method" alone, is an exposition in depth in which research has been expanded to its extreme limits.

Because of the diversity of its chapters, and in order to have the fundamental thought intact, it would have been necessary to command a transcendental style that carries the thought beyond the reality of the material. Alas, this is given rarely to writers!

Let the reader accept, in his appreciation "the glazing that invites the colors"; let him make use of it judiciously and with good will.

Let him recall, before opening this book, the words of the poet:

> "It depends on him who passes
> Whether I am tomb or treasure,
> Whether I speak or remain silent.
> It is a matter only for thee,
> Friend, enter not without desire."
>
> (Paul Valéry)

Paul Roës.

Prologue: Reflections on Music Through the Centuries

On a summer evening in Venice, two friends walked on the Piazza San Marco. They crossed the square and, passing the Byzantine Basilica on their left, approached the broad and limpid lagoons.

A diffuse, golden yellow light on the dreaming sea mingled with the shadow of ancient dreams . . . the light ripples splashed over the steps of the old Doges' Palace and broke against the hulls of sleeping gondolas.

The friends were silent. They had just concluded a conversation on a painful note. It was not at all a traveler's momentary ill humor which was the cause of their bitterness; the trouble was deeper. An abyss separated these two men. For once again, as if quite proud of it, one of them had reaffirmed that he lacked any musical sense whatsoever, and once more this boast jarred in the ears of the other, who was the musician. The latter had already repeated many times that absence of all musical sense is so rare that one never encounters any one who is totally deprived of it. Tired of repeating his own arguments, he was inspired to quote the phrase from Shakespeare where Lorenzo answers Shylock's daughter Jessica:

"You say you are never merry when you hear sweet music. Well,

> 'The man that hath no music in himself,
> Nor is not mov'd with concord of sweet sounds,
> Is fit for treasons, stratagems, and spoils;
> The motions of his spirit are dull as night,
> And his affections dark as Erebus:
> Let no such man be trusted.'"

—Act V. Scene 1, Merchant of Venice

Suddenly, a deep bell tone sounded from the campanile of St. Mark's. The powerful vibrations of the sounding bronze surprised the two friends and swept away their disagreement. Their divergence fled as abruptly as the flock of pigeons which, in fright, left the Piazza.

The sonorous waves falling from the bell tower rolled out toward the horizon of the lagoons of the distant Adriatic where they seemed to spread out in the penumbra of time. For a long moment the city and the two men were enveloped by the vibrations, until the equally powerful sound of another bell, a tone lower, joined the resounding undulations. The duration of this eddying of sound was longer than that of the single

bell and, as if to accentuate this reflection from a distance, very tardily a third bell added its sound, a half tone lower than the second. The interrogative tone of this unexpected interval, strange and compelling, seemed to come from another world.

Powerful and mysterious was this *mélange* in which the vibrations reinforced themselves by fits and starts, sometimes turning back on themselves, vanishing towards the abysses of silence, only to take up again their fascinating flight toward the borders of the sea.

For a long time these bronze voices filled all space, then . . . little by little lost their vigor. The waves of sounds were interrupted by momentary, hesitant cessations . . . the sounds scattered more and more . . . several more straggling vibrations . . . and then followed the wonderful silence . . .

The musician, returning to reality, addressed his friend.

—What did you say? You said something?

—I have just experienced a very strange sensation: those sounds from the bells suggested to me a retreat into time as if I were living in a distant past, centuries and centuries ago.

—I am surprised, and happy at what you say; I am delighted that you have just discovered in yourself what I call a profound musicality.

This strange revelation, this lesson so unexpected was to be continued a few hours later. The scene was a loggia giving out on the Grand Canal. In front and above them was displayed a majestic spectacle of myriads of stars which sparkled in the warm night. A voice in the shadow asked:

—Would you mind talking to me a little about music?

—On the contrary, in this atmosphere a conversation about music is quite appropriate. One has a much freer spirit in these surroundings than in the city when music might be discussed after a concert. The sensation that you just felt during the vibrations from the bells of St. Mark's: tell me, was it personal in the strict sense of the word? Or were you inspired to reach into infinite space, "outside of time"? It was afterwards, in the immediate silence, that you realized you had experienced what you called a "retreat into time." When I termed your sensation, caused by the sounds of the bells—their intervals and their relative durations—a profound musicality, I meant that you had been touched by the deepest, the essential part of music, which is universal, cosmic.

—This recalls a remark of Paderewski which you quoted to me recently: "If music is of all the arts the most readily accessible, the reason is that it is cosmic rather than cosmopolitan."

—Liszt presents this idea in reverse when he says: "The supreme harmony of the Cosmos is reflected in the harmony of the spirit." It

would greatly benefit those who study music seriously, if they were introduced into this domain, but the manual work preoccupies them so much that they forget to rise again to the source.

" Please, let us first take a look at the principle. To clarify, let us begin by emphasizing the distinction between "music" on the one hand and "the art of music" on the other hand, as it is done in the German language by means of the words *"Musik"* and *"Tonkunst."* The music lovers, amateur and professional, are most usually interested in "the art." I am not referring to teachings of the historians when I say that the majority of melomaniacs do not know that side of history which has nothing to do with the knowledge of facts and events, but treats of the history of the interior evolutions of music.

—This astounds me that you speak first about its history and not, first of all, of its thrilling attraction.

—All this forms a part of the history of its intrinsic value. Let us select out of the immensely diverse types of music throughout the world, the one closest to us, which is occidental music. In order not to exceed the scope of our discussion I shall only mention its ancient origins, such as the customs of primitive peoples who invoked by their rudimentary music the good spirits and thought they were providing protection from evil fate. This sorcery, though more in use among Orientals—these manifestations of superstition—also penetrated the customs of the early Occidentals. In a scholarly book by J. Combarieu, The History of Music,[1] there is a very profound chapter on this subject of "incantation among primitive peoples."

—I know that among the Spartans there existed a musical institution, the Katastasis, about six centuries before Jesus Christ. In the cult of Apollo, they sang about the spiritual ascent of the soul, and about confidence in the gods "who make order reign in the world." On this subject the historian Otfried Müller[2] gives ample commentaries.

—Let us begin with the Greeks and follow the evolution which came about between their time and ours.

" In their mythology, the splendor of the gods was conceived in terms of human beauty; their gods were created after man's image, attributing to them human virtues and weaknesses. Their world was a completely happy dream of man made into god.

[1]Jules Combarieu, History of Music, Vol. I. Armand Colin, Paris, 1953.

[2]Karl Otfried Müller, *Geschichte der griechischen Literatur.* J. Max, Breslau, 1841. Also A. Heitz, Stuttgart, 1882-1884. (A French translation was published in Paris in 1883, by A. Pédone.)

—What a marvel was Plato's revelation which reversed this ideology! What illumination!

—Isn't it astounding that only much later this evolution appeared in the most incorporeal of arts, music? But one realizes the wide range of a wing-beat only when perceiving its destination. It was revealed to us by Christianity; from then on, art virtually enters into the domain of spirituality. But let us not digress too far from our subject.

—I follow you. . . . with regret. Let us return then to the time when philosopher-legislators saw above all in art its influence on customs.

—Yes, but let us look more closely at the foundation of their philosophy. They considered music as the essential element of man's inner life, understanding on the one hand the complexity of feelings which constitutes his *subjective* nature; on the other hand his perceptions of the external world, the *objective* element.

—The consciousness of this duality exists and always will, in each human being. Within it is mingled his intuitions, his beliefs, the mysteries of religions.

" The whole of Greek tragedy is an illustration of the duality in man: constantly seeking the relationship between the two natures, and manifesting the oppositions within that duality.

—Thus it was with conceptions concerning music that for the ancients had very strict ties to the verbal art. Yet for them music furnished grander aspirations. The spoken word alone, enriched with every imaginable nuance, could not attain the intensity of melody. Song, translated by the voice, which is the organ inherent to the body and thus naturally close to the spirit, was considered as the ideal expression; and essentially must express in the most striking way the emotions and sensations of the heart. Thus with the Greeks, the choral song above all became an exclamation from the depths of the soul.

" Quite different was their estimation of the use of musical instruments. These appeared to them a nonhuman expression, that of nature. Not only could these musical instruments never attain the beauty of the human voice, but their easy virtuosity was to be feared; also their luxuriant caprices, the rapidity of which would exclude emotional sincerity and truth.

—All of these ideas conformed to their mythology wherein Pan was the personification of nature. Nietzsche, in his studies of ancient tragedy, penetrated further into the antagonism of man's two natures, opposing the "Apollonian," internal or subjective nature, and the "Dionysian," the reflection of external or objective nature.

—Yes, but this definition of Nietzsche's, perspicacious as it is, was made in the light of subsequent studies . . . For centuries, this duality exercised a great influence. The distinction between sacred and profane music was even more accentuated. Later the church, in its partiality for song—like the Greeks but from another angle—made certain that the influence of musical instruments was kept out of the liturgic rites, and the Gregorian chant flourished in all its splendor.

" But in the fourteenth century a bridge is thrown across the current which separated the two elements of the ancient conception: we see appear, as by enchantment, in paintings of the primitives, of Ghirlandajo, in the frescoes of Fra Angelico and of other painters, sacred and celestial instruments for adoring God. We will never completely understand what inspirations, what changes of attitude toward the musical instruments, caused such a transformation of opinion. Their entry into art, thanks to the primitive painters, later guided Monteverdi, Bach and Beethoven. Thereafter, the instrument was always an integral part of music.

—Now, if we declare, with relation to Bach, Buxtehude and their predecessors such as Monteverdi and so many others, that the instrument is there to serve music, on the contrary we see later, particularly since the beginning of the seventeenth century, music in the service of the instrument. It suffices to look at pictures of this epoch to reveal that instruments were found in the salons only to convey charm and elegance . . .

—. . . as was said later by Stendhal: "Music is only a drawing room amusement."

—The letters of Mozart relating his sojourn in Paris bear this out bitterly. We may admire the contrapuntal style of dance forms so seductive to the ear in the compositions of Couperin and Rameau, but relatively speaking, these composers cannot be included in a stream of thought which concerns the profound meaning of music.

" Continuing this train of thought, the music of Monteverdi and his contemporaries, more than a century previous, was something different. To what degree was this a source of inspiration for Johann Sebastian Bach? With him, appeared musical works in which grandiose conceptions surpassed the means of expression which the instruments of his era offered. The piano did not yet exist, the organ had not yet attained the perfection which one knows today; only the stringed instruments had already reached maturity.

—What do you think of the concerts where the works of Bach are interpreted on the piano?

—Your question is of great importance. We can consider them as the first manifestation of transcription, which proves that music is stronger than the means applied to its realization. This translation by transcription is comparable to the supremacy of the spirit over matter. The great interpretations are expressions of the substratum of art; they become staggering when, suddenly, the interpreter succeeds in concentrating here the slow evolution, the vibrating message that reaches us through time. They furnish confirmation of the interior evolution of the art of music.

" Under the baton of Wilhelm Furtwängler, the development of the instrument's value, its application idealized and perfected to the point of revealing the clear manifestation of its destiny, is one of the marvels of our era.

" Suppose we now visualize the theatrical music of the eighteenth and nineteenth centuries. The human voice was degraded by making it a veritable tool of virtuosity, and the false exaltation shone in a thousand facets. It was no longer an expression of profound emotion as existed in the ideal of the ancients.

" It remained to Gluck at first, then to Mozart and to Wagner, to effect the reform which was to return to the voice the expression of its own nature. This was a battle against superficial virtuosity, empty of meaning. To restore to the voice the clarity of the spoken word, to attenuate an excess of orchestral effects, was the first stage of an evolution based on the principle of twenty centuries previous.

" The revived ideal attained its highest expression in the theatrical work of Wagner. It did not stop at purifying the dramatic art but was the first to consider, in opera, music as the conceptual element of the drama, the stage becoming, in consequence, a secondary element.

" It suffices only to hear *Parsifal* in order to grasp the point at which the principles emanating from the original duality find here their perfect resolution. Wagner often emphasized this transformation in his assertions with this conclusion, that opera is a "means" and not an "end in itself."

" Has it never occurred to you that this thought is indeed the principle of his operas? If it were not so, it would be perfectly unbelievable and ridiculous that a hero, after having been mortally wounded by a sword, continues to sing for a quarter of an hour: it is the soul which sings and not the personage on the stage.

" Everything in his operas is symbolic: characters, helmets, costumes, scenery; all are "means" and not "ends in themselves."

—Your exposition progresses as tranquilly as the night advances towards the day.

—Do you feel that we are in the main stream or above it? . . .
" I suddenly think of the collection of correspondence between Wagner and his friend Häckel, that I lent you.

—I am now reading it. There are some very amusing pages. The joy of Wagner is touching when he found for his orchestra "already six first violins and ten seconds," and where he announced: "many people will be coming from the suburbs, among others a certain Nietzsche."

—When one thinks of the upheaval this meeting created! One also sees with what modest means Wagner contented himself. Nothing yet presaged the heavy performances which often obscure the beautiful transparency of his scores. We seem to forget that the *Siegfried Idyll* was played for the first time by a small group of musicians . . . it was a morning serenade. But let us go on, so that we may arrive little by little at the end I have in view; do you know the work of Debussy?

—I can say . . . only in part.

—Your modesty is certainly . . . honest. But you have undoubtedly admired the transparent sonority, the particularly Latin clarity of *Pelléas et Mélisande* and of his symphonic works. In *Pelléas et Mélisande,* it sheds on the text of Maeterlinck, poet of the North, sometimes a diffuse light, sometimes the whiteness of the skies of southern countries.

—Isn't his music a reminiscence of ancient times?

—Beware! The word "reminiscence" signifies for many, a "return."

—Would it be then, this music Nietzsche speaks about when he dreams of an ideal . . . "a super-Mediterranean music"?

—Remember also that the master idea of Nietzsche in *Zarathustra* was a consuming doubt which he expressed in a formula, a true menace that weighs on all life, and consequently all the arts: "That which is great in man," he said, "is that he is a bridge, and not an end in himself."—and then his discouraging idea—"That which one can love in man is that he is *a transition (Uebergang)* and . . . *a fall (Untergang).*"

—I begin to sense your objective . . . You believe in all evolution that is an elevation, whether in life or in music.
" I have followed you well when, in developing your thesis, you have spoken of the revelation brought to you by the paintings and frescoes of the primitives, and through your profound reverence for the names of Giovanni da Fiesole—the admirable Fra Angelico—and of Ghirlandajo, you have wanted to say that the miraculous in art is its renewal by its spirituality.

—I will lead you to a better understanding of it with a word from Chesterton, who, in speaking of the splendor of the thirteenth century, defined this renewal in an admirable way: "This was the era where life created life."

—What contrast between these words and those of Nietzsche, where *fall* is the last word!

—It is clear. That which the Greeks have taught us must be merely a point of departure.

" If one does not understand that their ideas were carried further and higher by Christianity, and how much their conceptions of the song were enriched by those qualities which are the essence of the plain chant in the middle ages, expanded in the works of Josquin Des Prés, Orlando Lassus, Palestrina and Monteverdi; if one does not want to recognize the decadence of certain music in the seventeenth and eighteenth centuries and, during the epoch of decadence (oh! paradox of history!), the restoration by Buxtehude, Bach, followed by Beethoven, Bruckner, Mahler and the poets of the Lied such as Schubert, Wolf and Mahler; and if one does not see the decadence reappear in the major part of our modern music, the chaos, the absence of love for the beautiful which are characteristic of our epoch, one is obliged to repeat, to the diapason of this discouraging abomination, the word of Nietzsche: "That which one can love in man (as well as in art) is that he is a transition and a fall . . ."

—That which is destroying in Nietzsche, and that which has finally destroyed him is the contradiction that motivates his thoughts and by which they are consumed. But, to return to the constructive evolution, I must tell you that as much as the tracing of the interior evolution of music has fascinated me, I am still perplexed concerning your opinion about modern music. You are surely inconsistent when, after having described the marvelous renewal, the redress which was produced during the seventeenth and eighteenth centuries, you leave so little hope for our era. This attitude appears severe to me, if not unjust.

—Precisely. I do not exclude any possibility for redress. I commend progress even in following the interior evolution of music, but it is not sufficient to want to create something new above all. When it obeys an exterior influence, the will to create is incapable of giving an eternal value to a work. That which marks the composer in the first place is the impulse within, the absolute necessity to create. It is the flame of this necessity which makes the eternal value of masterworks.

" Listen to the impetuosity of a Berlioz and the tragic accent of the Sixth Symphony of Tchaikovsky. Although differently conceived, these marvels and those of Mozart live side by side with the works of Beethoven, of Wagner, of Mahler and of Debussy and so many others. How could

one otherwise explain that their works are always and universally appreciated? You see very well that, to judge our era, I do not place myself on a level of personal criticism. In support of the general idea which is at the source of all the arts, I have made a comparison with the actual conceptions.

" Some will say that Beethoven, in his lifetime, was ignored. This disregard is not at all a criterion. The chord of the ninth in his *Eroica* Symphony, misunderstood and considered as false in his time, has since become the most poignant expression that music sets forth. Thus, the intrinsic value of a work escapes, owing to erroneous opinions and incomprehension of the times.

" Diepenbrock, in his *In Memoriam* to Mahler, evokes the thoughts of this composer: "That which I desire is not at all riches, nor honors, nor fame, nor even admiration, but simply Love." And Diepenbrock adds: "This love we have not yet given to Mahler, except only parsimoniously." Then he cites the verses of the Second Symphony:

> "With the wings I have conquered *(errungen)*
> I am going to fly. I will die to live."

" It is certain that one still finds in some music of our era, the impulsion of this love: life creates life.

—You envision then the possibility of a new expansion of music?

—Obviously: although the fashion of an era can smother life, injure the soul, it cannot annihilate them. Grains of wheat found in the tomb of a pharaoh were sown and the harvest was prodigious. What I have wanted to demonstrate tonight is the indestructible force and the intrinsic value of music.

The two friends were quiet for a moment . . . then the musician resumed:

—Do you feel the magnetism of this immensity? The starry night invites a concentration of ideas. Day is propitious to their expansion. Night shows us the infinite above the shadow, the day clarifies space.

—For you musicians, nothing is static, you even live beyond the passing mode.

—All the evolution of music is opposed to static thought. The working musician constructs in sound and silence. He compares, sorts, chooses, perfects, and in such a way assembles the matter of sound with a view to the spiritual; the artist is on his true course when, with the aid of sonorities, he shows the flight of constructive thought towards its origins from where beauty emanates. The work, whether it be a sculpture, a painting, or a composition of sound waves is, in short, only a receptacle

of the spirit that animates but does not identify it. It is impossible to seize materially what we call the beauty of a thing since it is fluid, moving, diaphanous, settling nowhere. Those who perceive its presence would like to seize it. They approach the subject in order to penetrate the mystery, and search in the vibrant air for the "pentacle" of the secret of sound, but they have not seen it, they have not heard it.

" The rustle of leaves in the forest does not cling to the foliage, a reflection on the water does not fix itself, the flight of the bird leaves no trace in the blue.

—We are indeed far from the formula of Leibnitz: "Music is the arithmetic of the soul that does not know what it counts."

—Interesting theory but purely unwarranted. Many a philosopher, in wishing to penetrate music, halts at the very gate of its mystery. And what consequences this limitation allows! Nietzsche, in his inclination toward music, discovered there the releasing of powers which could cause suffering by their abundance, or rather, he found there the intoxication and evasion for those who suffer from the impoverishment of life.

—And besides, in contradiction with these ideas, he insinuates that philosophy is "the universalization of the suffering of a single being." It is the road to despair.

—But the spirit, and by consequence music, rejects abandonment to despair; if not, why should one write any more?

" Because it is more comforting to think of those overburdened with suffering who have still found the strength to sing the "Ode To Joy." Next to the names of Beethoven and Schubert many others stand.

" In the midst of their illustrious group, one stands apart, whose greatness is less understood because he gave so keen a tone to his ideas that numbers of his contemporaries—and even artists of following generations—were distrustful. They admired only his dazzling talent. However, he considered this as only secondary. All of the irritations and even the hatreds that a musician can rouse as a defender of the universality of art and of Christian thought, fell upon the man who fought openly during the greater part of his life for such convictions.

—You mean to say . . . Liszt?

—Indeed I do mean Franz Liszt. He entered the musical world as an astounding pianist, he left it a more astonishing composer, leaving more than twelve hundred works. Of those composed for the piano we know but a small part, most often badly interpreted, since neither as a man nor as a composer was he truly understood, no more than were in consequence his conceptions of playing. His glory faded as the laurels;

forgotten at the end of his life; his death brought little notice. It was announced laconically at Weimar that the father-in-law of Richard Wagner had just died. Schubert's Lied: *Fremd bin ich eingezogen, fremd zieh' ich wieder aus* (Stranger I came, Stranger I depart), is as significantly, as grievously true for the composer of this Lied, as it is for Liszt.

—What a strange paradox . . . those who are a light for so many others are doomed to solitude.

—It is often the destiny of the elite; in giving all, they remain alone. So human thought proceeds on its way. The mission of the artist is a continual sacrifice; his work, like himself, is assailed with pain. The idea that leads him is for him the only source of joy. One rarely calls to mind that the glitter of concerts reflects nothing of the birth of a work, nor the pain that it admits of, nor the happiness that is given the composer in the flowering, blooming of his inspiration in the silence. Living in the world of music, one forgets often the source from which it comes.

" Music is by nature transcendent. Perpetually in spiritual evolution, it is the eternal token, testimony of the most profound in man, who searches consciously or unconsciously an expression of the highest in himself. It is also, for us pilgrims, during our mysterious passage on this earth, an invisible, but indeed present companion.

—This evening, enveloped in the vanishing sound of the bells, I was overcome by a strange sensation, and I do not know whether the conversation that we just had has not shaken me more greatly.

—Would it not be you who, by the effect of your emotion, led me to formulate my ideas in a way quite different from my usual habit? The more one inclines to the mysteries of existence, the more one studies art and particularly music, the more one sees that they follow the same path. The destiny of music, like that of life, is an eternal ascendance.

* * *

The two friends sensed that the subject of their conversation would soon be exhausted and that another was forthcoming in their thoughts . . . but it was already late. The clock of Santa Maria della Salute, whose blurred silhouette they could perceive opposite, had just sounded the second hour. In the shadow of the loggias of nearby palaces voices could still be heard, but in murmurs, an agreeable contrast to the clamor of hoarse voices of the gondoliers going up the Grand Canal, black mirror of the moonless night of Venice.

PART I: THE INFLUENCE OF FRANZ LISZT

CHAPTER ONE.
The Legacy of Franz Liszt

"all that ascends converges."[3]

Would it not be to the honor of humanity if posterity preserved only the good memories of its chosen few?

Alas, man is far from respecting that which is the closest to his heart. The image of the great composers is blurred quickly in the twilight of time and, because of false legends, that which remains is often unrecognizable. Moreover, their works little by little lose their original sense by time's attrition and by the deformation produced in the minds of those who come after them.

In the domain of creation as well as in that of appreciation, music, like all the arts must be based on its own nature. In denying its laws, it can doubtless become something else, an art which must be named something other than music. Beethoven gave an eloquent warning against such deviations, when he wrote as epigraph to the *Pastoral* Symphony: *Mehr Empfindung als Malerei* (More Feeling than Description).

Not only does this recommendation reveal the fundamental sense of his work, but even more it defines the principle of all music of the past as well as the music of the future. Forms change but not the principle.

* * *

Music differs from the plastic arts in the fact that its works must be constantly recreated. It depends therefore on interpreters. Their task is enormous. Among the multiple problems to be resolved, there is that of penetration, in the highest sense, of the music itself; thereafter, the comprehension of the work played. It is necessary to put forth, not a personal technique, but a much larger technique for the rendering of a work of universal importance.

To acquire this technique, it is necessary to know thoroughly its evolution, just as its artisan has conceived it, and consequently to have more than a vague idea of the personality of a composer who, by his grandiose conceptions, has largely exceeded the limits of a personal technique. The whole man was engaged in those researches, deductions and conclusions, so that any wrong idea of his personality will prevent us from following him on his road. We must understand him in his role as a pilgrim.

[3]Words of the Reverend Father Pierre Teilhard de Chardin.

If Beethoven, in the advice he wrote preceding his *Pastoral* Symphony, has formulated a fundamental law of music, we can say of Franz Liszt that he formulated a principle of playing the piano, one which is fundamental for the execution of all works written for this instrument.

Considering first of all, Liszt the person; what does one know of him? Do we know him better than Chopin? If today Chopin came to life and gave a recital of his works under a pseudonym, we might risk hearing remarks like, "he is a wretched pianist, and especially he plays Chopin badly."

One might say of Liszt: "This poor pianist may well disguise himself as Liszt, he has understood nothing; nothing goes out from this diabolic virtuoso who breaks at least five strings per evening; his calm is a real sham and above all—oh! how slowly he plays Bach, much too slowly! The only thing that makes me think of Liszt is that he *looks* inspired because he holds his head well back."

But those who know, query their friends: "Have you noticed the duration of his sound? One does not hear its birth, the sound is there with no noise of percussion. As a Dutch poet has said: 'the snowflakes are there, and we did not see them come.' What atmosphere that gives! There is a wonderful plenitude of sonority that leaves no trace of noise during the rests. . . . Leaning his body and his head slightly back, he seems to want to listen to himself from as great a distance as possible . . ."

This evocation of Chopin and Liszt reaffirms the idea that any false image in which we have framed an interpreter disturbs our capacity to listen to him well, and to appreciate fully the value he gives to the music he plays. Often a simple unkind suggestion, an unjustly accusing critic, a point of view presented in a biased and wounding manner, more even a constantly propagated hate, can delude the opinion of too easily impressionable men to the point of leading astray the minds of entire generations when it concerns a man who was really an illustrious personage.

If one accepts as true the descriptions of Beethoven that his biographies give us, one can only see in imagination the deaf musician leading his orchestra without hearing it. Having no psychological nor physiological knowledge, they present his deafness as an accepted fact, relying on the Heiligenstadt Testament, written in the middle of his life. Was Beethoven almost deaf so young, and completely deaf at the end of his life?

All the same, one is astonished by the fact that he is never mistaken in the choice of his chords, the delicate balance between the different sonorities of the instruments reenforcing the harmony.

If it is true that a blind man never runs into an obstacle, it is because he "sees," thanks to the digital and epidermic sense. Does not the musician hear, apart from his sense of hearing, by means of the same organs which guide the blind man? And then, do we know all the secrets of the "inner ear"?

It would therefore be more equitable if the biographers would add to their commentaries the fact that the deafness of Beethoven did not prevent him from hearing and reproducing the most inconceivable nuances; in consequence we would listen with fewer false conceptions to the last quartets and symphonies, which are an example of auditory sensitivity.

If the historians and the illustrators would represent him as a little less choleric, would not see in him a raging eccentric, bare-headed, hands clasped behind his back, walking across the forest with its idyllic little stream, they would avoid the ridiculous. And finally, if they would describe him as less fierce than "having the muzzle (sic) of a lion, fearsome jaws that could crack nuts"[4] the admirers of music could better understand the "dolce" character of his compositions. They would listen, less troubled, to the symphonies that bring joy to men. This discouraging portrayal therefore has nothing in common with the composer of the funeral marches, where the oppression of sorrow is followed by a consolation that can only be conceived by someone who knows the fullness of joy.

Often it must be said, the lack of comprehension of the narrators attenuates their responsibility, but it also happens that their talent as writers simply impairs the person they describe. Their consciences submit without scruple to their ambitions; they think only of their pretty story, designed at all costs to strike the imagination of the reader. Thus they ruin or coldly kill an illustrious personage. Yet, the responsibility of those who exercise a decisive influence on public opinion is enormous.

Everything considered, there are many things to say to those who have contributed to the obscuring of opinions concerning one of the greatest figures that the history of music has known: Franz Liszt.

To recall a picture of Liszt, there is absolutely no need to repeat the anecdotes of his biographers. We readers certainly know these little tales, most of which make us smile and shrug our shoulders. Nevertheless, some exist that appear to us necessary to mention.

A whole voluminous literature intended for any who wish to see an eccentric in every artist, and directed equally to young and easily influenced students, a whole library full of biographies, contain a *mélange* of anecdotes, not one of which takes into account the psychological factor that gave birth to them. These meaningless stories have brought prejudice not only to the person of Liszt, but also to the personality of Liszt. They have damaged the appreciation that ensued.

Misappreciation has become fashionable. False legend has given the grotesque portrait of a degenerate apostle of romanticism. It depicts an extravagant virtuoso, gathering laurels that he purchased for his own cause; it imparts to his concerts a taste of the circus. It pictures a demolisher of pianos, engaging them in veritable battles, with strings breaking en masse. Heinrich Heine colors the truth by telling us, "He was the scourge of God for Erard pianos."

---

[4]Romain Rolland, *Vie de Beethoven.* Hachette, 1922.

According to his chroniclers, the over-excited imagination of his fans had taken the form of collective hysteria.

So here, the whole lot of storytellers show us the image of a rover of the drawing room, a mountebank in a cassock. With these traits, Liszt appears as the incarnation of a degenerate romantic of the nineteenth century. Nevertheless, we wish to draw attention to the excellent biography of Guy de Pourtales,[5] and a perspicacious study by Amédée Ponceau.[6]

The caricaturists outdid themselves in following with an extreme zeal the fashion of the times. Caricature is a powerful propaganda; often pure ridicule lacking any humor, it speaks to men who have preference for distortion rather than reality.

Doesn't the figure of Don Quixote emerge in the deformed ideas of those who are incapable of recognizing the grandeur of man? Hasn't the genius Cervantes presented the world with an immense tragedy of human interpretation that sees folly and burlesque in the superior man? Some, happily, recognize in this figure its stature, despite all the ridicule, and his tall silhouette stands erect on the summit under a luminous sky.

* * *

Let us for an instant return to the biographies of Liszt, by quoting a single typical example. In this description, what is striking is the entanglement of contradictions. Many biographies contain so much that is illogical that we cannot help thinking that these statements must be false. It is not our intention to accuse all these authors of bad faith; far from it. That some of them were, is evident; the reader will judge for himself by referring to the outrages coming from Heine; but above all it is their inability to understand a figure like Liszt that causes so many errors. Let us look at our typical example before giving a psychological explanation.

In a chapter, "Liszt as Idealist," from the biography entitled Liszt, author Constant van Wessem[7] addresses dithyrambic eulogies to his hero, the master of Weimar. Thus this writer intends to refute ridiculous and improbable stories, too widely prevalent. But he does it in such an untoward way that a perfectly grotesque portrait results . . . In forcing himself with grandiloquent phrases to render him homage, he draws the following conclusion from his account: "Was Liszt a charlatan who did not know his own capabilities?" This illogicality would be harmless

---

[5]*La vie de Franz Liszt.* Ed. Gallimard, Paris, 1927.

[6]*La musique et l'angoisse.* Ed. La Colombe, Paris, 1951.

[7]C. van Wessem, Franz Liszt. pub. J.-P. Kruseman, The Hague, 1927.

if the interrogative phrase was not one of these facile means to kindle the reader's imagination. But his biography becomes dangerous when he recalls several sarcasms of Heine, the poet of *"vergiftet sind meine Lieder"* (poisoned are my poems). The most venomous of the acid jeering is really this one: "Liszt has chosen his hobby-horse in all the riding-stables of philosophy." And van Wessem, without taking account of this, naively pursues his own idea: "Liszt has never done anything without profound religious thought." It would have been so much simpler on the part of van Wessem to explain why the poet pursued Liszt with his hate. Religion was quite simply the cause.

Quite another explanation must be given of the incomprehension that characterized the general opinion, among Liszt's contemporaries as well as with the following generation. Even among those nearest to him, including some of his students, he was often misunderstood. One of his disciples understood him profoundly; that was Moriz Rosenthal. We must give Rosenthal credit for having communicated, without keeping anything secret, his rich experiences to all those who had the pleasure of approaching him.

Member of a group of students of which, besides him, the most famous were Eugene d'Albert, Alexander Siloti, Emil von Sauer and Frédéric Lamond—all of quite different characters—Rosenthal appeared among them as the most objective observer. Self-confident, he approached Liszt in a complete freedom of spirit. He told with pleasure how much his master appreciated this independence: "Above all no imitation; it is better to find for yourself, after mere suggestions on my part," he had the custom of saying. A perfectly free admiration resulted from it.

Rosenthal did not have Liszt's religious conceptions; for this reason, his words of admiration were strictly objective, the least contested. Another reason for his objectivity was the ease with which Rosenthal developed his technique. Effort never obscured his spirit. "The vexation of an obstacle" he said, "begins when one imagines that it is insurmountable." Provided with the easy technique of a Godowsky, having a keen sense of analysis and synthesis, he belonged for a long time to the elite of pianists. His memories, rendered precious by the intimate contact that he had with Liszt, merit more attention than writings of the whimsical chroniclers.

One day, speaking of his master, after remaining deep in his memories for a moment, he supplied a key to the enigma of this misunderstanding of which Franz Liszt was the object: "Liszt was not at all a man like others. One always felt that his suggestions came from a mystical thought. He saw further than we did, and when he spoke, his thoughts were so well-considered that he gave the impression of seeing with the eyes of a creator . . ."

Doesn't this testimony bring to the light of day the inaccessibility of this man, who was judged by the men of an era to which, in reality, he did not belong? Liszt only belongs to the romanticism of his time because of its profound meaning: a powerful current where life quenches its thirst and nourishes itself at its very roots.

Since the world began, there has been romanticism. The encyclopedias generally situate romanticism in the nineteenth century, the period of the predominance of sensitivity and imagination over reason; in other words, of the reign of individualism—while adding that it honored the Christian religion and paid homage to all great beliefs since time began. All religions have known and recognized that life is a passage to a better life. This is to declare the inherent dissatisfaction with the tragedy of human life. One often forgets that the deep movements of generations do not identify themselves with the name of a transitory epoch. The romanticism of the nineteenth century had its purity and its decadent vogue. Even today, one wants to see in Liszt a child of his era; in reality he abandoned it from his twenty-fifty year, the date of his first important compositions.

To have a clear idea of the inward turn of his thoughts, we must read these lines in his work on Chopin[8]

> "Let us learn from him whom we have just lost; to reject all that does not hold to the elite of art's ambitions; to concentrate all cares upon the efforts which leave a deeper mark than the fashion of the day! Let us reject for ourselves sad times of futility and any artistic corruptions in our surroundings; all that is not worthy of art; all that does not include the quality of durability; all that does not contain in itself something of eternal and enduring beauty, that is enjoined upon art to make it resplendent for its own sake!
>
> "Instead of striving so much to attract crowds and their favor at all costs, let us rather apply ourselves, like Chopin, to leaving a heavenly echo of what we have felt, loved and suffered! Let us learn finally from him, and from the example he has left us, to exact from ourselves that which gives rank in the mystical city of art, rather than to demand from the present, without respect for the future, those easy laurels that, barely acquired, fade and are forgotten! . . ."

* * *

[8] Frédéric Chopin by Liszt. Breitkopf and Härtel, Leipzig, 1923, 7th ed.

Reading the writings of Liszt, his book about Chopin, his correspondence with Wagner and so many other eminent contemporaries, gives evidence of the admiration and generosity characteristic of a superior man. However, the qualification of a superior man demands more than these two affective qualities. Now, great rarity among men, Liszt harmoniously adds to his spiritual endowments an extraordinary intelligence. His intelligence and his affective gifts will always permit him to remain above the *mêlée* of events which his letters often echo.

Liszt possessed an almost infallible judgment when he found himself facing a musical work or a person with a profound sense of music. Intelligence, supported by a true intuition and verified by experience, made of him what one can call a superior man. Thanks to these qualities, he immediately discerned talent. His meeting with Berlioz instantly aroused his enthusiasm, to the great astonishment of his friends, who had quite opposite opinions from those of the master of the *Symphonie Fantastique.* To show this work to his friends, to "make them understand its worth," Liszt composed there and then a transcription for piano.

No musician has known and possessed so completely as he the music composed before his time and of his time. It is significant that Liszt was the first to play a sonata of Beethoven in public. The number of works that he transcribed or adapted, whether as a study for his own use or for concert playing, is counted in the hundreds. He penetrated also the inner meaning of these works in a totally new way, without losing sight, as Rosenthal said, of the least detail of the text nor the intentions of the composer.

To understand well the principle of a transcription, it is necessary to take into account that the idea included in a musical work goes beyond the form conceived by the creator. None can pretend that a composer, no matter how original, considers the form in which he has conceived his work as being the only one possible. The three different overtures of *Leonora* of Beethoven are a proof of this. However, the contours of a work traced on the paper are one of the conditions for its survival.

After these considerations it is permitted, while respecting the original form, to look for other means of expression for the same work. Evidently, the success of such a task is reserved only to the rare initiated. J. S. Bach has thus transcribed compositions of Vivaldi; among others he made a transcription for organ of a Concerto for violin and orchestra.[9]

We ask: does the essence of the definitive form of a symphony or other musical composition live as long as its script remains unchanged over the years, or does it live by the interpretations of generations which

[9]This concerto was long incorrectly attributed to Wilhelm Friedemann Bach.

keep it alive? In carrying our thought further, we are inclined to ask: is not a study around the original form the breath, *par excellence,* that makes it live? Should one, therefore, not refuse to reject *a priori* the principle of the transcription? Is it not best to praise these, provided they are made by the initiate? And to conclude: does the original form remain then so rigorously the only condition of the survival of a work? Does not the communion of geniuses also give the interpreter his *raison d'être*?

Liszt was one of these initiated. Imbued with the beauty and the grandeur of the works of Bach, he knew by experience the organ with all its immense possibilities. However, he preferred for certain organ compositions his own new means of expression that differed from those of all other pianists (with the exception of Chopin), by the sound prolonged, heightened by the contrast of different touches: *non legato, mezzo legato* and *portato,* interposing the secondary voices to point up the "canto" or principal theme. We choose the word "interpose," not only to indicate polyphony in the music but also to characterize his manner of playing, quite in harmony with it. The pupils of Liszt have all made the same observation; he gave less the impression of playing the piano than of setting his hands on the keys. The image gives the suggestion of a very differentiated distribution of intonations, which permit clear separation in polyphonic execution.

Busoni found, later, the exact word: *getrennt spielen,* which is translated less suggestively by "separated playing." The clarity obtained in the separation of voices, as well as their multiple intonation, naturally led Liszt to transcribing organ pieces for the piano.

The enormous volume of sound that this pianist knew how to draw from his instrument wonderfully suggests the power of the organ, and often the sonorous sounds of the organ seemed even surpassed, by means of the ingenious writing and the strength in the contrasting intonations.

However, above all, it is the enhancement within the polyphony that often makes the transcription superior to the original. This is realized with difficulty by the best organists when the same hand plays more than one theme, which is frequently the case in the preludes and fugues of Bach.

The ideal of clarity, pursued for as long as music has existed, doctrine of the ancients, of composers of the Middle Ages and of those of today, is thus fully attained. This prodigious work done by Liszt had a continuation on a larger scale.

Ferruccio Busoni continued with a whole series of masterworks, some more important than others, such as the transcription of numerous works of Bach. It is necessary to have heard and played the preludes and fugues, the toccatas, the Chaconne and the choral preludes, to get a clear idea of how the original work can be enhanced by putting into practice

a profound knowledge of the composer together with a knowledge of the means of expression of the instruments in question. Busoni, like Liszt, was supremely intelligent; like Liszt, he played all the literature of music. He had equally as grandiose a playing at his command, even though the source of their inspiration was not the same. Despite the fundamental differences between Liszt and Busoni, the one a mystic—the other a Renaissance man, Busoni, by his intelligence, drew so close to Liszt's intentions that he became his most brilliant and devoted interpreter.

To commemorate the centennial [1911] of the birth of Liszt, Busoni conceived a project so audacious that the most daring among the musicians called it a folly. He wanted to honor the master of Weimar by a demonstration that had never been dared: concentrating in a cycle of six concerts his essential compositions, known and unknown. Alone at the piano, Busoni filled these six evenings with this gigantic program, which he modestly qualified as a very limited summary of the whole of the master's works. To represent the orchestral compositions and those for organ, Busoni added some of his own transcriptions. By way of an introduction, a preface appeared in the program, the words of which were a veritable provocation to the antagonists. Here is the text of it:

> "Liszt," the octogenarian Grand Duke Charles Alexander of Weimar said to me one day, "was such as should be a King."

And the text continued:

> "He was a king by virtue of his spirit, his commanding presence. Moreover, he was an artist by the happy union of his talent, his intelligence, his determination to work, by his constant pursuit of the ideal. As such, he possessed all the characteristics of the truly great man. Great because of the universality of his art, by the three periods of his creations, by the constant research to the end, the enigma of his talents, the magic ease of his executions, the magnetic effect of his art; all of these factors contribute to making Liszt a legend. He aspired to the heights, to ennoblement, and to detachment. Only a great soul tends toward greatness; only a noble soul tends toward nobility; only he who has known how to detach himself from this world can have a real conception of freedom. His name is inseparably united with the piano, which he elevated to the rank of nobility, so that it might be worthy of him."

This portrait of an illustrious personage astonished the Berlin public. This Liszt, described thus, was completely unheard of, and the numerous

antagonists were dumfounded. However, hidden in corners of the concert hall, his enemies returned each night.

In leafing through the program, people were stupified. A whole series of unknown works was announced and the pianist, in a few words, excused himself for giving in the course of six concerts, only a relatively small part of the whole of the master's compositions. As for musicians, most of the great names of this epoch were present. One could recognize the best known composers and pianists among the audience in Beethoven Hall, which was an acoustical marvel. The imperturbable Bernard van Dieren, little known up to that time, seated beside Schoenberg, said laconically: "It is time this should be known at last!"

The triumph of Busoni was so considerable that people already talked of a general conversion to the ideas of Liszt, but alas, the duration of this enthusiasm was short. The war [1914] was drawing near, and after this scourge the spirit of the musical world was totally changed. They preached then in Central Europe *"die neue Sachlichkeit in der Kunst"* (the new objectivism in art), a conception which has become in our days the replacement of all sentiment by the mathematical construction of the robot-man.

The history developing around "Music" is not identical, far from it, to that of the interior evolution of music; this last is, by its nature, universal and eternal, independent of temporal events. The great compositions reflect, first of all, an immutable principle; the echo of confusion in the world has only a secondary influence. Also this influence only manifests itself slowly in works. Schubert said he never was disposed to translate immediately the sorrows that had come to him. It is therefore natural that the composer finds in his art a refuge from the vibrations of reality. It is his school of wisdom, and according to these precepts he allows everything to mature.

Would Liszt complain about the alterations undergone by music in the midst of a world's confusion? He would say, "let us apply ourselves, like Chopin, to leaving a heavenly echo of what we have felt, loved and suffered."

Beethoven, in the middle of sorrowful events and at the peak of his misery, found consolation in this formula: "Music, like every art, is founded upon spiritual beauty, every creation of beauty bringing a new degree of spiritual perfection." [10]

The testimony of Liszt was constant devotion to this ideal. His example is a light which can never be extinguished, because the source is in itself.

---

[10] *Goethes Briefwechsel* (Correspondence), page 325. *Ed. note:* This must be one of the many German editions.

Those who close their eyes to avoid seeing it, can consider that it is as independent of them as the sun is independent of the rays it casts on the earth! May those who see his splendor find there an ineffable joy, as the words of Dante proclaim:

> "He who holds to the bonds of this world has not yet heard all music . . ."

The detachment from his own glory is perhaps the most beautiful legacy that Liszt has left us. He communicated his inspiration to others, without taking pride in his influence. There is not one opera of Wagner where one does not find the traces of Liszt's music, written long before.

Liszt gave Wagner, whom he admired as none other, his musical findings with the same generosity that he displayed in providing him with financial support, without ever claiming the least credit. He considered music as a gift of inspiration and not a possession of the artist. To create a beautiful thing was for him to shine forth beauty, in which no artist should take pride that he accomplished this by himself alone. His arrogant epoch could not accept Liszt's convictions. It did not forgive him when, at the age of sixty years, in full physical and moral force, Liszt definitively renounced all glory and all of his triumphs. The Parisian world, whose ideal was "to make a show," saw in this renouncement a defiance.

But everything became for him a more and more intense concentration, an internal enchantment; he had understood that existence has no meaning until one knows how to forget self. Thus he loved life, which he felt within himself, that he perceived in his fellow men, and in everything; he understood that only he who loves can admire. Liszt, as friend, defended his contemporaries while sacrificing his own self. When he wrote to one of his friends struck by fate: "Admiration has an opposite: hate; enthusiasm has a reverse: outrage," he certainly did not think of his own destiny. The last words that he pronounced were again to express admiration in homage to his friend Wagner. At the doors of eternity, his final word, transported in ecstasy: "Tristan . . ."

The testimony of Liszt is that of a generous genius. Let us remember his words about Chopin. Is not the mystical city of art, about which Liszt tells us, the supernatural world that Huysmans evokes by the admirable words: "the mystical soul . . . the gift of the superhuman exile"?[11]

While the materialists refute these thoughts, the mystical being leans toward them and directs them beyond the materialistic conceptions while

---

[11] J. K. Huysmans, *En Route,* Tresse & Stock, Paris, 1895.

perfectly understanding their sense. The inequality of these two tendencies is always the cause of profound divisions.

Liszt's comprehension of the different facets of life is the reason why his epoch did not understand him, any more than ours. It is a fact that the great mystics—who so profoundly influenced Liszt—were also great intellectuals. This should perhaps open the hearts of antagonists. Liszt himself had passed through all the stages of the road that leads to this conversion.

In the minds of the adversaries of spirituality an admission arises even now, and the day will come when the legacy of Liszt will lead to the full recognition of his universal ideas and his ideals.

CHAPTER TWO
The School of Weimar

When, at the beginning of the twentieth century, Rudolf M. Breithaupt published his book, *Die natürlich Klaviertechnik*,[12] "The Natural Technique of the Piano," the musical world had reached the pinnacle of great interpreters.

Liszt's school at Weimar not only developed the talent of numerous pianists, directly through Liszt's own pupils, musical descendants and friendships, but also exerted great influence as a meeting ground for the artists.[13]

Pianists were not the only ones to give this era its splendor. It was reflected among other instrumentalists, in the art of conducting the orchestra, and through singers of the *Lied.* Many great artists threw a vivid luster over this century's beginning.

While these interpreters were enchanting the concert audiences in this era when the musical world knew the glory of the greatest interpretations, the theorists of piano playing accomplished, besides their imposing performance, their work of research. They were numberless, and here we see one of the most important, Rudolf M. Breithaupt, publishing the most astonishing, the most pessimistic of declarations in this outrageous paradox: "Of all the six thousand pianists who follow the courses of all our institutions every year, only one good performer appears every five to ten years; among this small number there is a genius every fifty years!"

One could take this as a joke, but such was not at all his intention. Did this veritable funereal oration contain unhappily a sinister prophecy? Did this cruel phrase sound the knell for tens of thousands of students and innumerable professionals who with unremitting effort, consecrate life, fortune and health in the hope of achieving, according to their ideal, the interpretation of works that they love above all? The exaggeration of this statistic being admitted and the pessimism proven, we would like to probe what is justified and what is unjustified in such an assertion.

Breithaupt will remain the most important of all the theorists of his time. In his treatise of approximately fifteen hundred pages, he deals

---

[12]C. F. Kahnt Nachfolger, Leipzig. *Ed. note:* Published in 3 parts (1905, 1909, 1919). Part 2 was translated into French, Russian and English.

[13]*Ed. note:* See Amy Fay, Music-Study in Germany in the Nineteenth Century, Ch. XVII-XXIII. Dover Publications, Inc., New York, N.Y., 1965.

exclusively with the question of earlier and of contemporary systems, while adding a kind of synthesis according to his own ideas.

Precursors of Breithaupt's theory began to establish some rules for a system of piano playing. By advocating muscular development as a requisite apart from the instrument and the music, their theories separated from the practice of Chopin and Liszt. We draw attention to these first symptoms of separation between theory and practice. Chopin taught that the essential condition for any contraction [muscular] is a stable support which permits the shading of such an action. "The fingers are only pillars and all action follows in due order," he said. And long before this, these great practicians, Liszt and Chopin, had established the fact that all technique must be constructed on the stable base which is found under the keys.

The error of many theorists of piano playing proceeds from the fact that they build systems around their own individual physical features. But the physical characteristics are different for everyone. The piano offering an equal base for all, the conclusion is imposed that a system which is not built on this given fact has no general authority. Libraries contain hundreds of theoretical treatises, some of which call themselves "method." However, a method must contain something more than personal experience; it supposes an initial base on which it is constructed. Among the voluminous collection of systems of piano playing, we have no knowledge of one that has a better right to the name of "method" than the discoveries of Liszt and Chopin, transmitted orally or by their writings.

Their method rests on an initial given fact: the necessary base to piano playing is the table which is found under the row of keys. To this fundamental idea are joined two physical phenomena: gravity and the arrest of the fall on the fixed table. *These phenomena being known, we can construct of this initial given set of data a system of ordered actions, according to a method that sets the elements in a logical progression and leads to the only possible result.*

Liszt reached this unique conclusion. He planned a book of three volumes, the first of which was completed. Unfortunately, this precious document was lost by the unbelievable negligence of one of his pupils. What renders this loss so great is that Liszt had not only found the definitive solution for piano technique, but also possessed all the gifts to solidify his ideas. Endowed with a clear style, he had an innate sense of deduction: he felt constantly the necessity to verify and refine his thoughts, to test them by tracing back to the starting point, so that, with the aid of certain hypotheses, he could prove he was right.

Obviously the publication of this book would have dissipated many misunderstandings among the theorists as well as practitioners of teaching. But Liszt left us another document: his works for piano that contain

just as clearly what his treatise on technique could have explained.[14] It appears at first completely improbable that these works as originally printed could bring to light the very action of his playing. Nevertheless, in many places, the original phrasing and fingering irrefutably show this action. We will return to this fully in the following chapter.

Besides his own writings, we possess the testimonies written or transmitted verbally by his disciples, which will also be explained in the same chapter, entitled "The Birth of a Method."

It is certain that Breithaupt knew of these testimonies that the pupils of Liszt transmitted to us. He visited them from time to time to wrest their secrets from them. We have the echoes of them and it is a fact that this curious theorist wanted to impose his own ideas rather than to listen to those of others.

Because of his own loquacity, these visits brought him nothing. So then he simply attended the concerts of his interlocutors.[15] There he drew his astonishing conclusion, in an almost ironical way, in his book, after his extensive study of all the existing systems: "Seen objectively, the technique of Liszt is doubtless the greatest, the most fluid, and at the same time the easiest played, of all the systems of virtuosity." What a happy discovery after the sinister quotation earlier in this chapter!

What became of Liszt's school after the glorious epoch when his disciples still shone? For a time it practically disappeared from Western Europe. But there have been signs of a revival of the Weimar spirit.

In Italy the influence of Busoni is felt in many cities of the peninsula, at Rome, Florence, Bologna and Sienna. Twenty-five years after his death, Busoni, at first forgotten, seems today to come back to life in the hearts of his compatriots. They also remember in Tivoli that at the Villa d'Este the aged Liszt lived among them.

The Russians have appreciated in their own way the lesson of Weimar. Siloti lived a long time in Leningrad where he trained many students whose worth we are acquainted with. Alexander Siloti, who molded Sergey Rachmaninoff, was not only the favorite student of Liszt, but the latter chose him particularly to propagate his teaching. Russia has had flourishing schools: at Kiev, which gave us Vladimir Horowitz, at Moscow,

---

[14]*Ed. note:* An edition of Liszt's technical exercises was published in 1971. Liszt Technical Exercises for the Piano, Ed. Julio Esteban, pub. Alfred Music Co., Inc., Port Washington, N.Y. In his foreword, Mr. Esteban refers to the "mystery" of these volumes that were never published by Liszt, but by Alexander Winterberger, one year after Liszt's death.

[15]*Ed. note:* Arthur Schnabel told his pupil Konrad Wolff that, after a concert early in this century, Breithaupt, whom Schnabel had never met, rushed backstage and exclaimed: "You play with shoulder participation!" Later the two got together and discussed technique.

and at Leningrad, whence now and then young pianists come who greatly astonish the audiences and the contest juries of the great cities of Western Europe.

If those in authority do not realize what kind of teaching these young pianists receive, the problem of good teaching becomes not only delicate, but difficult to solve. However, in this domain, all is reparable. Let us begin by glancing at another aspect of the school of Liszt which is not in the domain of technique, but in that of psychology, and we will soon find the reason why the outcome of success is today no longer comparable with that of fifty years ago.

It is certainly a fact that theories cannot replace the fruits of practice. In practice there is a basic factor, the living example that can be given only by professors who are at the same time accomplished pianists. And this is not all. It is necessary that the playing of a master be suggestive enough to awaken the self-teacher in the pupil. This process seems paradoxical. But if one studies this question intently, it becomes clear that the last phase of the conception of an act is the idea that the apprentice himself makes of it. Since first infancy, the human being does a thousand things instinctively. We show a child how we walk; but it is not by pure imitation that he learns how to walk; it is from his own stock that he draws the means to accomplish it. His impulsions achieve the act. Thus, naturally, we possess the aptitudes of a self-taught being. We assuredly do not admit that the musician should be deprived of this faculty. Now, it is evident that a surfeit of imitation—a phenomenon too well known in art—will extinguish this precious initiative.

Liszt taught by suggestion in advising: "Follow yourself the road that I can only point out to you."

Is this manner of teaching anything else but awakening the sense of self-teaching in the student? Liszt thus joined the experience of acquired understanding to the wonder that a young pianist feels vibrating in himself.

Diepenbrock, after having fathomed the secrets of composition, recalls the predominant element of this art when he says: "I am self-taught, for a god has poured forth his songs in my spirit."

Respecting this humble recognition that distinguishes every great artist, there are happily some professors who know that persuasion can never replace suggestion so fecund. They direct their teaching towards this natural and marvelous liberty that permits the student to find himself.

It often happens that a young being is enraptured by the discovery of a harmony which breathes new life into a melody many times heard. Encouraged by judicious teaching, he becomes conscious of being able to give form to his thought, and at this moment his spirit will naturally go towards his master.

What prudence is necessary on the part of the latter, when the predilection of a youth is revealed! If, unfortunately, acquired knowledge has made him forget his own first enthusiasm, the master can no longer effectively guide his young friend.

Great pedagogy is in constant evolution, technically as well as mentally, without losing sight of the starting points. Under these conditions, a prodigious contact can be established with mutual advantages. No master worthy of the name denies that teaching is a double school from which he profits as much as the talented student. Little by little, the harmony between the master and the disciple intensifies and enlarges. Soon a new ambition awakens in the spirit of the young man. His study of the instrument will lead him inevitably and naturally to an overestimation of his manual work. It is the crucial moment. It is a matter then of showing him the life-giving source that nourishes each performance of value. A new phase of instrumental instruction begins: to make known the beauty of song that finds its most perfect expression in the *Lied.* No school is more useful for the instrumentalist than the knowledge of this art which is the ideal form of the expression of the soul.

The intrinsic value of this fundamental means of expression is in its intensity and at the same time its sobriety. Speech is the indicative element in it. The music, and above all the melody, are most intimately and most thrillingly the messengers of our emotions.

There is no doubt that Liszt was inspired by his admiration for the *Lied* of Schubert. More than one hundred *Lieder* were transcribed by him for his own use, his own delight. He did not know the songs of Hugo Wolf, nor the marvels of Gustav Mahler, nor the last works of Richard Strauss, but we find already some precursive accents of them in all of Liszt's works. One discovers there the solitude of intervals of repeated thirds of Mahler, the mystery of the strangely fleeting meditations of Wolf, as well as the severity of the sad prophecies of the *Lieder Not* and *Morgen* of Richard Strauss. Liszt was of one spirit with them, already far from the brilliant interpretations that numbers of instrumentalists believed to be expressiveness par excellence.

But there is something else hidden in the execution of the song, also of great importance, that we wish to consider closely. It contains the faculty that is linked with our reflections on self-teaching. The formation of the voice is in the last analysis the result of the singer's own experience. We can give him indications for placing the voice, but no one can indicate to him in a precise way where the actual basis of the most perfect ease is found. If the pianist has at command, as we have seen, a fundamental element, stable, but independent of him, on which he can build physical action, this is naturally lacking in the vocal art. Because of this absence, the quest of the singer will be more intensely concentrated on his own

experiences. Deprived of a comparison from outside, the formation of his voice concerns him only, with his intuitions and the suggestions of his master.

Where does he find the source which feeds his way of singing? In the beauty of the work which he interprets. Between the understanding of music and its performance occurs self-teaching. The one teaches the other, and all the worth of the singer comes from this harmony. Finally, the ultimate school is the quest of beauty. The blossoming forth of great singers, men and women, is spontaneous, as among the flowers of nature. Their tradition consists uniquely of the fact that they sing the same *Lieder,* the same works.

The song concentrated in the *Lied* has thus become a universal school, and one can never say often enough that the *Lied* must be known and then thoroughly studied by all those who play an instrument; if not they will remain incomplete interpreters.

After having evoked the ambiance of the school of Weimar; after having considered the mediocre influence of the theorists on the great interpreters; and having revealed also the value of self-teaching and the possibilities of awakening and cultivating this precious gift, we wish to study a third element of Liszt's teaching. He was a protagonist of synthesis; he was above all a builder. What is found in all its splendor among violinists, namely a solid and long tradition of a true confraternity, unfortunately was lost to the world of pianists after the death of Liszt.

The principal reason why the playing of pianists has sometimes been deficient resides in the incomprehension, and therefore the misunderstanding, of the way of playing of Liszt and Chopin. In their day, the historian Kleczynski found himself confronted with an enigma when he saw Chopin play.

"I suppose," he wrote, "that it is a manner rarely used and doubtless exaggerated by his pupils?"[16]

We understand his astonishment at this playing, stripped of any physical gestures, even in the most animated passages, while the massed sonorities were of unheard-of abundance and force of penetration. One heard a sound of extraordinary duration, blown out like that of a wind instrument without the impact of its inception, and similar to the sound produced by a long draw of a bow (in spite of the early type of piano with parallel strings).

[16]Jan Kleczynski, *Chopin's grössere Werke.* Leipzig, 1898. *Ed. note:* As Kleczynski was about age twelve when Chopin died in 1849, it can be doubtful that his statement was based on having heard Chopin play.

All of this was an enigma too for Clara Wieck, who was quite confused when she heard Liszt.[17] It seems that she had been dumfounded by the calm of his playing. Instead of sitting erect during the vehement passages, "he slumped in front of his piano." Regarding this observation, Liszt looked for a very low posture in order to properly attack his *fortissimos,* and thus he drew himself down.

Liszt explained his posture at the piano to his disciple Clark in the following manner:[18]

"You have never noticed that I am seated low, and far from the clavier, for, if my size is relatively small, my upper arms are longer than most pianists'."

Clara Wieck played in the manner of Thalberg, where the fingers are raised high, and her incomprehension while watching Liszt play is thus clearly understood.[19]

Clark cites a description that George Sand made of Thalberg's position before his instrument:[20]

"Thalberg, large-bodied, sat down on an ordinary chair in front of the piano. He had such an awkward position that he resembled a chimney. The elbows as well as the hands formed a right angle. His fingers had the appearance of being bent angularly and the hands gave the impression of being a hammering machine where they rose up and pounded down. Each sound he produced was cold and dead."

Liszt said to his friend Clark, on the subject of these angular movements:[21]

"With a pianist, you can recognize by the position of his elbow, bent or stretched, whether or not he has discovered the secret of my free action. But, even the arm stretched out can lead to error, for in this case the pianist may be seated high and thus his arm is automatically stretched and extended. Extended in this manner it presents an unfortunate phenomenon. In effect, an angle is formed between the arm and the surface of the keys, and thus the approximately horizontal line between the shoulder and the ends of the fingers has become impossible. The cause of this evil resides in the high position before the piano."

However, what remains inconceivable is the fact that one century later many technicians have not yet understood it. On this subject a little story,

---

[17]*Journal de Clara Wieck.*

[18]F. H. Clark, *Liszt's Offenbahrung* (The Revelation of Liszt). Ed. Viweg, Berlin, 1907. Page 94. *Ed. note:* See Frederick Horace Clark in Appendix A.

[19]Liszt was twenty-one years old at the time.

[20]F. H. Clark, op. cit., page 73.

[21]F. H. Clark, op. cit., page 94.

amusing enough in part, frankly disconcerting in another way, concerns the author of this work. Having published the first short volume,[22a] in a series of writings bringing to light some characteristics factors of the playing of Liszt and Chopin, we had the idea of taking a copy to one of the present masters of the piano.[22b] After thanking us, he said: "What you write on Chopin's technique is curious; I have just discovered a manuscript written in his hand and I must tell you that I find myself in the presence of a way of playing diametrically opposed to everything I do."

A little disconcerted by the discovery of this rough draft, he refused to show it, saying that the document figured in the exposition "George Sand and her Friends," at the Polish Library in Paris. In fact we found it there, carefully displayed behind glass. Before leaving the master, at the time of our first visit, we had warmly recommended that he read the essay we had written, cited above. In response, he wrote us a charming letter congratulating us on our "ingenious hypotheses." However we had advanced proofs. We understood his embarrassment at the time of our visit at the Polish Library. In examining the rough draft of Chopin, we could read there a phrase in which he spoke of points of support, an idea developed in a former document of Chopin, *La méthode des méthodes,* advocating the non-activity of the fingers. It is evidently the absolute contrary to the recommendations that the master in question gives in a collection of notes, where he counsels raising the fingers as high as possible. We can consider this little story as the testimony of lack of interest in this question: "How did Liszt and Chopin play?" If one reflects that Chopin practiced exactly, but less completely, the same playing of which Liszt had revealed the secrets, one remains astonished by the fact that such immense values for teaching thousands of pianists meet such negligence and even opposition. Nevertheless, it appears that, very recently, certain professors (we do not know for what reasons) are suddenly changing the fundamental rules of their teaching without giving any studied explanation, so that the students ask the "why" of it. We have several echoes of their advice: "sit lower," "do not raise the fingers nor the forearm nor the wrist," and the students wonder why they are taught the contrary of what had been recommended up to the present.

But it is better, even if the professor does not know what reason to give, that he nevertheless gives the advice, for it could be that one day the student might find the solution himself. It is perhaps to awaken in the student the self-educator, were it only by the absurd.

[22a]*Essai sur la technique du piano.* Henry Lemoine & Co., ed., Paris, 1935.

[22b]*Ed. note:* This master was identified by Marie Stuart de Backer as Alfred Cortot.

It would be much simpler, and above all much more efficacious, to acknowledge the value of Liszt's teaching to his students who gave stunning proof of it at the end of the nineteenth century and at the beginning of the twentieth century, and to strive to penetrate his lucid and wise spirit.

The universality of Liszt's revelations is concordant with clairvoyance; it is then logical that this school be reinstalled there where Liszt lived and taught, like his friend Chopin. But their admirers, convinced of the value of these revelations, have not all the necessary courage to confront the difficulties that a conformist world imposes on them; let us cite then in brief.

There already exist centers where out-of-date practices have been discarded; where it is understood that before all study the taste for music must be awakened and developed; that theory is deduction and not a point of departure; that playing the piano cannot be acquired in applying a technique meant for instruments which are precursors to the piano.

To mention one of these new tendencies where the teaching is in the spirit of the only sane and great school, we cite a recent short work on musical education by Roger Cousinet.[23a]

One finds here valuable directives for teaching the young. The experiences of Maurice Chevais, as well as the conclusions of Roger Cousinet, deliberately move far away from the constraints of theory; the counsel we find is oriented towards the joys of the first impulses in a formula: "First music, then studies."[23b]

With reference to teaching, there are some who, while having acquired high qualities of expression thanks to perspicacious studies, do not possess the precious gift of communicating to others; this talent is sometimes missing in the best pianists.

The survival of a school depends not alone on its intrinsic value. Its life is more fragile than that of a musical work, for events around it can directly menace its existence. On the contrary, certain works are like a rock, resistant to all revolutions.

Listening to the *"Eroica"* Symphony today, one is struck at one and the same time by the creative force of Beethoven and by the present appeal of the work. The funeral march in which, during the *"fugato,"* the glory of the hero expands into every corner of the world, will be understood as long as there are heroes on this earth.

[23a]*Les Presses d'Ile-de-France,* No. 15, March 1953, Paris.

[23b]*Ed. note:* See Appendix B for other musicians that Roës commended in this part of the original French text.

When in 1854 Liszt wrote the preface of his symphonic poem *Orphée,* his anxiety unconsciously touched the acuteness of this problem; unconsciously, because he did not in fact establish his Weimar school until twenty years later. However, he spoke, in this preface, of the deprivation of the spirit and the destruction of barbarous war, imploring the aid of spiritual forces against these foes:

"Preached to by the purest of morals, taught by the most sublime dogmas, clarified by the most brilliant beacons of science, warned by the philosophical reasoning of intelligence, surrounded by the most refined of civilizations, humanity, today as before and always, harbors in her breast her instincts of ferocity, brutality and sensuality, which it is the mission of art to force to yield, to tame, and to ennoble . . .

* * * * * * * * *

"Grant, at least, that those times of barbarism and their stupid furies never return."

And the eternal poet ends with this exaltation:

"If it had been given to us to formulate our thoughts completely, we would have wished to express the serenely civilizing character of the songs that shine from every work of art, their urbane energy, their majestic grandeur, their sonority nobly voluptuous to the soul, their undulation, sweet as Elysian breezes, their gradual rising, like vapors of incense, their diaphanous and azured ether enveloping the world and the entire universe as in a transparent vestment of ineffable and mysterious harmony."

Thus spoke Liszt to his contemporaries and to future generations.

CHAPTER THREE

What Meaning Has Music?

I.

It often happens that amateurs and professional musicians ask themselves: "Can we understand music?"

The expression appears then as something too precise and one generally replies that individual impressions alone prevail. Understanding, we explain, belongs to our intelligence, while music speaks to other faculties within us, faculties that intelligence cannot grasp. However we all have the tendency to communicate our impressions in the hope of finding a response; to remain with our individual ideas does not satisfy us.

If one asks what this desire is, this need to love in the same way the same thing in a musical work, the question enters a larger domain. In recalling the assertions of Liszt and of Paderewski "that music is cosmic by nature, and that the supreme harmony of the cosmos is reflected in the harmony of the spirit," we begin to state them precisely.

Everything has a rhythm.

Around us, there is a constant and regular succession of days, seasons, years. All that happens in the universe and in nature around us is subordinated to the universal rhythm. Around us we see, in regarding events that seem at first glance dispersed, the regularity with which beings come into the world and die as if these events followed the swing of a great clock that tolls without our hearing it, inexorably marking time.

Within us, there is the rhythm of heartbeats, of respiration, the regular cadence of acts and events lived, sensed by our intelligence or by the causitivity of our emotions. In the morning one is disposed otherwise than in the evenings; day brings not the same ambiance as night; the sensibility of man registers and faithfully follows the rhythm of his impressions.

By us, there is the rhythmic regularity of our words, of our acts and our habits. We exteriorize during our whole lives what we have progressively conceived within us according to our momentary dispositions, or according to the impulses of our age; and if some attain wisdom, it is by repeated efforts to a cadence that others before us have followed. Discipline is forged following marked rules; decadence accentuates itself by stages, which we know by studying man's customs.

The artist, more than others, feels himself in the middle of this ensemble of rhythmic forces that inspire him to create, as Paul Valéry said with such simplicity: "Every man creates without knowing it, as he breathes.

But the artist feels himself create; his act engages his whole being, his beloved labour fortifies him."

If one really wants to distinguish the rhythms which we simply undergo from those we take active part in, one can appreciate the true value of the definition of the artist formulated thus by Liszt: "All of us who, by the grace of God, have the supreme honour of being artists, interpreters of eternal Beauty, chosen by nature herself, we have all become artists *by birthright as well as by right of conquest."*

In recognizing the existence of a master rhythm in the universe, in seeing that each thing around us, in us, and done by us, has a rhythm, in admitting also that the artist, a being sensitive to these phenomena, feels he lives in the middle of rhythms and currents, we have only accomplished the first stage of the journey that leads to the comprehension of a musical work.

Looking for the answer to the question "Can one understand music?," we want first to see whence the precision of speech originated and how far it goes.

II.

In the beginning, primitive man expressed himself by means of gestures and articulated sounds. It was the rudiment, the first notion of language which subsequently developed through experience of its efficacy. Gradually as the awareness of being understood increased, the primitive language became more complete and enriched, in order to respond to utilitarian needs as well as to the impulses that man felt within himself. The accompanying gestures, once the sounds had become language, little by little turned into accessories, as speech became autonomous.

Although subject to the natural laws, as all other things around him, man occupies a sovereign position in the middle of these currents by his reason, which is the faculty of knowing and judging; and by his intelligence, the faculty of knowing and understanding.

But there are no absolute demarcations, neither in man's spirit nor in nature.

First of all in substance. No material is found to be absolutely separated from other materials. Metal, no matter how polished, combines with oxygen; the two elements constituting water can enter into flame. In the same manner, there are transitions between the spiritual faculties in man. Often "animal instinct shows traces of intelligence."[24]

---

[24]Alexis Carrel, *Réflexions sur la conduite de la vie.* Ed. Plon, Paris.

Nevertheless, in spite of the absence of all absolute demarcation, each live being, every living thing, can accumulate power. We observe it in the concentration of light and heat; in the violence of the energies, of thunder storms and other phenomena of nature; in the force that makes the bud open; also in the birth of a being as well as of a thought. Speech, in its turn, possesses a nucleus of concentrated forces from which the sound waves issue to penetrate into our interior life. By this diffusion into space, it appeals to our intelligence and to our imagination in turn.[25]

This testimony of the power and the radiation of speech into both intelligence and imagination being accepted, we shall see more closely the significance and the faculties of the word "imagination." Because imagination is an important stage of the way that leads to an intelligent understanding of music.

III.

We distinguish matter from mind. Without further discussion we state that the orchestra that plays a symphony must not be confused with the symphony itself. The first is the effect, the second the cause. We admit that matter is a permanent cause of our sensory perceptions.

These are at the origin of our imagination. We distinguish in the imagination its reproductive faculty and its creative faculty. The first, inactive like memory, furnishes to the creative imagination the data of images conditioned to experience. The active and creative imagination possesses the faculty of comparing and abstracting the basis of the inspiration that art makes resplendent.[26]

The term "abstracting," in the philosophical sense as we use it, needs clarification. Abstraction is a process of the mind that considers involuntarily or voluntarily, through a process of separation, the faculties united in a tangible, visible or audible natural phenomenon. If a hard object is touched, mind distinguishes the hardness of the object itself; when snow is seen, its whiteness is considered separately from its substance; in listening to the sound of a bronze bell, the provoked emotion is registered outside of all consideration of the metal from which it came.

Admitting that this action of the mind may be provoked by the senses, we state that this process is only possible because of the absence of

---

[25]"Imagination," encycl.: faculty of representing to one's mind the visible and tangible world by means of thought. As used in its figurative sense as "fantastic opinion" [*opinion fantaisiste*], the word is outside of our considerations.

[26]Let not this expression "basis of inspiration" give rise to misunderstanding. Inspiration is a cause, whereas making resplendent by art is an effect. As clairvoyance is a "gift," it does not emanate from ourselves.

absolute demarcation; compartmental isolation would mean the non-existence of elements of transition.

Let us now project the phenomenon of the abstraction of the sound of the bell—of the metal that provokes it—on music in general. This abstraction, which takes place in our imagination in listening to music, consists in determining the musical sense of the sounds that penetrate our interior world by means of our organs (the ear and the sensitivity of the skin).

We far from know all secrets of the acoustics surrounding us. In spite of the research of the acousticians—Leonardo da Vinci was one of the most perspicacious[27]—the acoustical success of our concert halls depends, in spite of known laws, upon the intuition of the builders and to a great degree on chance. But, outside of acoustical spaces around us, there is *within us* a space for which the word acoustical is inapplicable by the fact that here there exists no delimitation.

We all know certain particularities of what we hear inside us without provocation from outside. The sounds that we hear in ourselves are completely different from those audible by the ear. If we observe the sonority of this interior voice or of the music that we provoke there, we realize first of all, that this metamorphosis winds back to silence. In this kingdom nothing sounds *forte,* not the slightest accent, all is muted there where the imagined sounds finish in *legato* fashion; all is heard there in a low voice and with perfect evenness. If one tries to hear a *staccato* sound inwardly, one must make an effort and borrow from the remembrance of what was heard outside. The more abrupt the captured sound is, the *sf-p* for example, the more difficult it is to hear it inwardly. Moreover, the conditions of time have changed. The duration of a piece of music that one can run through inwardly is not dependent upon time. We can reproduce inwardly in a short instant the summary of a musical work. If it were in reality played at this tempo, the ear could not register it because of its speed.[28] The change in the observation of time is of capital significance, both for the hearer and the interpreter. One could say that it is a fundamental factor of musical comprehension. The hearer undergoes this metamorphosis unconsciously, but his active imagination reacts; the interpreter is inspired by what he hears within himself; for him it is a source of realization. In playing the first note of an interval, he "hears" in himself already the curve that leads to the next note. The formation

[27]La salle Ibach at Düsseldorf, destroyed by bombing, was constructed according to his precepts. It presented the characteristic that, in all the rows of the parterre and in the most distant corners, the acoustics were of an astonishing clarity and perfectly even.

[28]This absence of time is found also in our dreams where one sees in the space of a few minutes a whole series of events.

of the next sound depends on this. Thus its sonority is formed in advance of playing.[29]

But the importance of this phenomenon of time-alteration within us is greater still. "*Tempo rubato,*" with which we want to deal at the end of the reconstitution of the method, finds its explanation there. *Tempo rubato* represents a relativity between strict exterior meter and indefinite interior time. The hearer transforms unconsciously; the interpreter does it consciously. When one hand plays in time, the other can transmit the performer's inner concept out of time. These two factors, strict time and the "outside of time," cooperate in making the hearer lose the notion of real time. The interpreter achieves this by intermittently consulting his perceptions outside and inside. Three means are at his disposal: *first,* comparing the inner and outer tempo; *second,* the fact that *pianissimo* seems at the same tempo slower than *forte; third,* the change in tone color.

As for the last two means, it is to be noted that great masses of sound proceed more slowly than those coming from only one instrument or only one voice. At the piano, chords come out more lazily than separate notes.[30] The masses of sound from a choir come to us more slowly than one voice. This slowness gives to the choruses of the Ninth Symphony of Beethoven, the symphonies of Mahler, and those of Bruckner, the distance of the spheres from which they seem to come.

As for different tone colors, it is proven that the sound of a bassoon or a double bass travels more slowly than that of a clarinet or a violin. The "*quasi trombone*" in the Chaconne of Bach-Busoni stops the tempo, which will be maintained by a sub-rhythm that the interpreter enforces. The phrase of the 716th measure of the Sonata of Liszt played "*quasi violincelli*" reduces the tempo to a slow resignation, while the same treatment repeated an octave higher "*quasi cor anglais*" (in the 718th measure) suggests a detachment of quite another nuance from one of resignation, as if the thought of goodbye wanted to anticipate the last chords in which little by little the Sonata, the epic in the life of Liszt, draws to a close.

The defenders of strict and metronomic beat, those who play only what is on the paper, consider it inadmissible to stop a tempo until it becomes an almost imperceptible progression in an evanescent *pianissimo,* and this in places where the composer prescribed no *ritardando.* They do not admit that at the end of the Sonata op. 109 of Beethoven, the trill stops almost totally, evaporating into imperceptibility, which permits the last entrance of the admirable theme—at first almost non-existent—to appear like a far-off vision.

---

[29]*Essai sur la technique du piano,* in Chap. IV. We insist upon the fact that the least technical difficulty impedes such a realization from the inside to the outside.

[30]The chord already presents the greatest rapidity of notes executed together.

In studying the score of Mahler's "Song of the Earth," we see that the succession, and often the astonishing simultaneity of certain indications, appear as a confirmation of the ideas we have just developed. At the end of the first *Lied* of the cycle is unveiled the secret between metronomic beat and of imagined time. We find in effect in the full score of the orchestra, beginning at number 45: *"a tempo"* for the execution of a sonority *"forte-diminuendo"* followed by *"sostenuto-crescendo,"* then, *"ritardando-morendo,"* while above the following measure, Mahler calls for: *"a tempo,* and take your time." It is after this that, in a *"piano"* for flutes, a *"double piano"* for harps, first violins and cellos and a *"triple piano"* for second violins, the transformation of strict time into imagined time is accomplished. From this vibration, abating and hardly perceptible, that seems to last an eternity, emerges the song of the tenor: *Dunkel ist das Leben* . . . tied by the hyphen of the slow grace notes *"morendo"* played by the violins and flutes in a continued *"morendo"* . . . . *ist der Tod.*

The adversaries of an inspired interpretation will some day realize that there is no strict meter except for the machine.

The phenomena of sound observed within us put into relief the full significance of the interval, which is the link that creates the relation *between* the notes.

As we have already said, the conviction of Mahler was: *Die Musik steht nicht in den Noten sondern zwischen den Noten,* that is to say: music does not reside in the notes but between them. The absence of the clean percussion of the sound, of its abrupt birth, leads necessarily to the *prédélinéation*[31] [French from the original] of the interval, of the curve that binds the sounds in us. Thus the thought of Liszt and Paderewski on the cosmic sense of music is found precisely.

It is in fact by the process of abstraction, faculty of our creative imagination, that the musical work, realized in space, enters our interior life. In these ideas are combined the thoughts of the two musicians, and the assertion of Kant, which we repeat: "Beauty is the reflection of the infinite across the finite."

IV.

We teach generally that the interval is the link, the curve-in-space between the notes. Let us now study the scale, in the light of what we have previously demonstrated. A scale is usually conceived as a monstrous

---

[31]*"Prédélinéation,"* stemming from *pré* and *dessin*, a philosophical term: having its course (or fate) by reason of its own nature.

exercise of a succession of notes, well determined, rapidly executed, without our hearing either the quick notes or the intervals between them. We call this prettily: pearly playing, a qualification exempt from the distinction between true and false pearls.

Let us take rather the succession of the scales in their ideal sense, as Liszt has written them in his Sonata in B minor, preceding the Fugue. The intentional slowness, the phrasing toward the leading tones, will not deceive the informed musician. He will hear a wandering melody. These scales, after a tumultuous episode that collapses in an oasis of meditation, search for a solution by following a thought. One could say that the sounds free themselves from their substance and lose themselves in the intervals.[32]

When a human being looks for a solution, he tries to make it satisfying and sure by getting rid of constraint. Would this be the triumph of reason, the gate of wisdom? These scales, at the end, lead toward the Fugue, which is an apotheosis of reasoning and wisdom. Such scales are then not a simple manifestation of a theory of notes, but they have a meaning of their own through their intervals which are ideally matched by the marvelous space deeply felt inside us. Because he was convinced of this, one master once said to his students: "My friends, there are no scales. Neither are there octaves, nor fifths, nor thirds, there are only intervals between two voices; it is as if I spoke to you and you answered me."

These reflections will be impenetrable to those for whom the fear expressed by Diepenbrock has become a reality:

"A time will come," he said in 1880, "when a word will have become the replacement for its own significance. For those who thus label the things of the soul, music remains a dead language."

During the same period, Mallarmé speaks with disdain of this *"bibelot* of resounding inanity," degeneration of great poetry.

We cite these references to mark the contrast between the coldness of materialism in art and the lively flame of imagination and affectivity.[33]

We progress to the most profound part of the mystery, that of the sound of the voice within us, as well as that of the sound around us. The latter originates from a nucleus of energy, and radiates in waves. These waves engender other sounds that are called harmonics.

---

[32]Clark relates in his book, cited above: ". . . then Liszt played me a scale, and I noticed that the motifs were grouped in many phrases, each motif neatly marked in the rhythmic liberty as well as in the dynamic execution. The notes were of a desired inequality, and grouped in curved lines. One had the impression that the motifs and the different groups were continual modulations."

[33]Affectivity, philosophical meaning relative to the affections of the soul.

Here is the series of overtones, or partials, which come from low C; while it is surrounded by numbers of other strings, those indicated below enter directly in vibration:

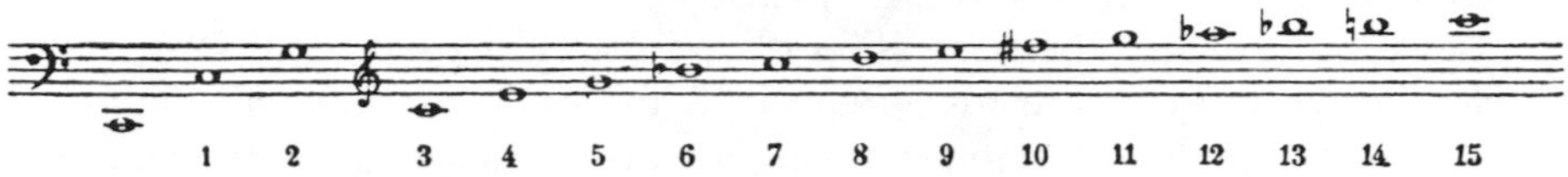

Each overtone is in its turn the fundamental sound of a new series of harmonics produced in the same order. Even though they are almost imperceptible to the ear, it is nonetheless evident that the retinue of sounds ramified to infinity makes contact with the most subtle fibers of the perception *within us.* What a multiple relation is established then in the depths of our imagination! In this domain, all of the transfigured vibrations meet, cross, and intermingle; in these depths, Rimbaud has drawn the association of the sounds of speech and of color: "A—black, E—white, I—red, U—green, O—blue; vowels, I shall say, some day or other, your latent births . . ."

Those who love music, as said at the beginning of this chapter, aspire incontestably to a common comprehension. One has a tendency to communicate impressions to others in the hope of finding an echo of one's own conceptions. Following the analysis just made, one has the right to replace the word "conception" by the word "imagination." And here is an admirable example of this imagination conveyed in an inspirational manner.

In an article entitled "The Apotheosis of Verdi's Requiem,"[34] Clarendon, the connoisseur and critic of art, wrote these lines:

> "I am blinded: this sun that reddens and darts forth its flames through the clamour of trumpets, it is the sun of the dead . . . What luminosity, what splendors, what lamentations! Here the flashing brasses, there the somber tapestry of the choirs, sometimes the simple voice of a frightened woman, shivering, pathetic and unadorned. Never has the human complaint made itself so vehement as with the pen of Verdi . . . There are Requiems that calm with their peacefulness—I think of Gabriel Fauré—this one consoles by its immensity. Thus does the mountain, and the sea, and the horizon . . ."

One is tempted after reading these words, to flee from a determining formula which is the aim of this phase of our research. After the marvels of poetry, as Rimbaud said, "scholarly penetration dampens our desire."

[34]*Figaro,* May 2, 1953

However, the precept of Beethoven gives us courage in this respect:

> "To submit oneself to the uncompromising laws and thus to direct one's own spirit in order to discover these laws, here is that quality which points to the one true artist among thousands of others."[35]

In conclusion, music first penetrates our inner world through the intermediary of the senses. Intelligence then associates a conscious perception to the spiritual picture that music has brought forth. The realm of the spiritual exceeds the limits of our exploration. If this area is entered, one then cannot understand music through the process of reasoning; however reason is able to find equivalents for mirages that music may arouse. With the initial semblance of a shadow that takes form, to a light that becomes clear, the emotional impress, ruled by sonoral phenomena, little by little finds its accurate expression within the domain of intelligence.

Nevertheless, the mystery of perception through intellect, as well as by emotional impact, remains valid. One needs only the experience of comparison in order to be convinced of this reality. Beauty is by essence elusive. Each sound contains something inaudible, each word hides the inexpressible. We cannot fasten, nor confine, the boundaries of what is beautiful in a line, even in finding the line beautiful. Said Baudelaire, "the marvelous fills us and envelops us like the atmosphere, but we do not see it."

The mystery of the irreal, illusive, seems at first more evident in music than in architecture, sculpture or painting. By its nature, music proceeds through the element of time, which allows a comparison between the successive elements.

V.

Any musical work contains similar parts, whether repeated or transformed. Moreover, there are in different compositions by the same composer, identical or varied fragments. Frequently a composer makes use of themes, ideas of a predecessor or contemporary, a practice sometimes mistakenly labelled as plagiarism.

Even though forms have evolved through the years for such designations as Suite, Fugue, Sonata and Symphony, composers have always reserved a certain liberty when applying the rules for such seemingly

[35] Beethoven's Letters to Bettina von Arnim. *Ed. note:* Bettina Brentano, whom Beethoven had met in 1810, married one of her brother's friends, the poet and novelist Achim von Arnim. Beethoven wrote many letters to her, often cited in his biographies.

arbitrary forms. Many sonatas of Beethoven are witness to this, including the two Sonatas opus 27 *quasi una Fantasia*, as well as the two Sonatas of Liszt, that in B minor, and that named *Fantasia quasi sonata*, "After a Reading of Dante."

It should also be observed that even the strict form of the fugue allows liberty in the development of themes, and that is when the free inspiration of the composer often produces the most beautiful moments of the whole fugue.

An example of free development of a theme in the sonata is illustrated in Beethoven's Sonata, opus 27, no. 2, arbitrarily called "Moonlight."

The first movement, Adagio sostenuto, begins with the identical notes, in triplets, as the last movement, Presto agitato, in sixteenths.

In the first movement, the initial note of the melody, G sharp, enshrouds the triplets, and this tone finds its echo in the Finale where it is heard twice in succession, *sf-p*, at the end of each ascent in sixteenths. Later on we will examine a number of similar treatments in Liszt's B minor Sonata.

To illustrate an analogy between different works of the same composer, we choose, among innumerable ones, the following example. Note the theme stated in the twenty-first bar of the Finale of the Beethoven Sonata mentioned above, then the striking similarity in the 117th measure of his Sonata, opus 111. The brilliant flash, in the first example, of impetuous youth is to become in the twilight of life a sorrowful musing, filled with acquiescent wisdom.

But notice the early theme is in the minor mode, the second in major!

In short, examples of composers borrowing ideas of predecessors or contemporaries are multiple, and through these revivals many estimable discoveries have been preserved for us. One hears in the introduction to the last movement of Beethoven's Ninth Symphony, the theme of

Mozart's *Offertory*. This theme dominates the entire final movement of the Symphony:

Beethoven, 9e Symphonie

plus loin:

Some reproach Mahler for his supposed plagiarisms; they forget that in these moments his music clarifies the profound meaning of the original, in giving occasionally a dreamlike aspect to what he transcribes. Has he not given, in his *Lied von der Erde*, a new significance to a motif that we find in many of his predecessors? To cite only one example, this particular type of motif in *Der Abschied*. Beginning as a simple embellishment, it expands to an elevation of the soul with Beethoven's *Kreutzer* Sonata; and then in his *Siegfried Idyll*, to an enveloping tenderness (as Liszt, previously, in his Sonata in B minor). It becomes with the touch of Mahler the eternal return to self-reflection, in using it as a link between life and death. We hear it three times, accompanying the song of the text of Li-Tai-Po: *Dunkel ist das Leben, ist der Tod*. The first time, played by the oboes and clarinets, the second time by one oboe, and finally by a lone flute, accompanied by violins. We read the following indications: "*lentement, expressivo, laisser du temps, morendo . . .*"

One of the most moving examples illustrating the adaptation of works between composers is certainly the great *Metamorphosen* of Richard Strauss, which is evidence of his long and prodigious life.

This work for chamber orchestra reveals, among several of Wagner's thoughts, his themes of the Guild of *Meistersingers*. From the beginning, we hear the descending tones of the funeral march of Beethoven's *Eroica* Symphony. All is developed in an atmosphere that is dramatic, at the same time with a grandeur that Strauss had never before attained.

Only once . . . at the end, appears the entire phrase of the funeral march, terminating in a chord so poignant, that one's emotions are almost beyond containing. By thus uniting two of the greatest works of different composers, Strauss has found a touching expression of the hope underlying sorrow. This should be one of the few pages that Debussy would have added to those he judged sublime, which according to him, were so rare that they would barely cover the surface of a table.

The few examples just given represent a generality. One could continue infinitely to disclose such similar characteristics.

The essential, outside of intrinsic value, is the process of *comparison*. This process of comparison shows us the following relation: if, under the sway of magnificent sounds, creative imagination finds in itself its expression within the domain of intelligence, it follows that the same process can be traced in the musical score.

In order to close the circle of this group of ideas, we refer to the beginning of the chapter. Everything has a rhythm, not only the phenomena *around us*, or *within us*; for rhythm manifests itself as well in our acts. Let us now examine the relation between this manifestation of rhythms and the operation that proceeds in the creative imagination that we have just studied.

One has the desire to understand the spirit of another individual. The gait of a walk, the quality of a voice, the glance—undisturbed or concealing, can reveal what we seek to find in him.

If rhythms such as these lead toward a better understanding, how much more then does the music of a composer guide us toward his intentions, which are included in the work itself! We have illustrated the differences which occur when we reproduce the sound of a work in our mental ear, within our interior world. Furthermore we have established that the artist, being sensitive by nature, is more than others influenced by the rhythmic forces which govern all of us. It is by consequence evident that, being creator, the artist concentrates the whole of his being into what he creates; it is therefore logical to conclude that the written music is the conception, not only of his feelings and of imageries roused within him, but of all the rhythms which manifest themselves around, within, and by him. *Our faculty of comparison will unite* all that is included in the work with what operates within our own imagination while hearing it. At this point the comparison plus the experience fulfill each other, and the rhythms reveal themselves to us through these two elements. It becomes clear; the more we know of musical literature, the more we study the scores of a composer, the more this language will reveal to us the profound meaning of the works.

VI.
The Sonata in B Minor[36]

When in 1853 Liszt wrote the final measures of this work which remains, among his compositions for piano, the most perfect and the most important, he had reached the age of forty-two. In order to have a clear idea of its worth, we wish first to trace the three roads that converge at the time of this achievement.

At the debut of his career, the young Liszt was the dazzling virtuoso to which no pianist of his time could measure himself. His playing was of such ease that no physical effort could impede the realization of his intentions as a musician, penetration of which identified him with the image of his conceptions as man and artist. Soon he was prepared to put his new technique in the service of the most profound musical expression. Whether at the organ[37] or the piano, a new "sound" made itself heard; an unknown world was revealed to wondering connoisseurs.

Toward attainment of this hitherto unknown perfection, Liszt was enriched by his professional experience. Very young, even at the age of fourteen, he worked on the first outlines of the twelve *Etudes d'execution transcendants*; at age twenty on those of the studies of Paganini, all definitively finished in his twentieth year. Innumerable identical works followed and his two Concerti in E flat major and in A major, begun in 1848, were so to say, the last experiments before the creation of the Sonata. All of these preliminary technical compositions served to deepen and broaden Liszt's method of writing as well as his means of execution.[38]

During his youth, in order to acquire more professionalism, he wrote transcriptions and variations on the works of Rossini, Spontini, Berlioz and Bellini; when he was thirty, he had finished the transcriptions for piano of six of the nine symphonies of Beethoven. This gigantic task was preceded by the following of his own compositions: *Première Année de Pèlerinage* (*Suisse*) and *Sonate après une lecture de Dante*, this last in 1837.

---

[36]We use the C. F. Peters edition (Leipzig), this being a faithful reproduction of the manuscript in the possession of Emil von Sauer who, in his youth, had studied this Sonata with Liszt.

[37]It is to be noted that certain organists of today astonish by the clarity of their playing *non legato* that binds perfectly the sounds in the space of a church. We remember the eminent organist Joseph Bonnet.

[38]One particularity in the execution of Liszt's works during the epoch of great interpretations at the end of the nineteenth and beginning of the twentieth century, was the absence of all impression of repetition in themes and figurations; each renewed passage had the breadth of unconstrained insistence.

Meanwhile, in addition to these two converging roads toward perfection of the Sonata's construction,[39] technically as well as musically, we distinguish a third, sunnier one that outshines the other two: the road on which the spiritual light was his guide. At eighteen years of age, Liszt suddenly interrupted his brilliant career as virtuoso, an interlude that he later renewed by going to Rome.

When the young Liszt, in full glory, turned his back for the first time on the world that lauded him, to retire into religious contemplations, it provoked first a stupor mixed with irony, which soon bordered on hate and outrage.

Twice during his lifetime Liszt very nearly entered the Franciscan Order. At last he became a member of the *tiers ordre*, and wore the cassock after his fifty-fifth year; he was never ordained priest. He remained in the world while remaining faithful to his religion; his talent as musician furnished him a compensating inspiration. The first testimonials to his religious convictions are the following compositions: *Pensée des Morts*, written at age twenty-four, a small work that fifteen years later was included in a collection of 10 pieces entitled (Lamartine) *Harmonies poétiques et religieuses*. Initially assembled in seven notebooks and dedicated to the princess of Wittgenstein, these works carried the titles: *Invocation, Ave Maria, Bénédiction de Dieu dans la solitude, Pensée des Morts, Pater Noster, Hymne de l'Enfant à son réveil, Funérailles, Miserere, Andante lacrimosa*, and *Cantique d'Amour* (1834-1853).

It requires just a glance to see what prodigious disciplines in three different areas were achieved by the time Liszt composed his Sonata in B minor. The worth of the work must give evidence to this. In its form of one movement alone, unknown then for a sonata, it combined the highest symphonic expression with the solidity of the epic, while the whole is conceived in a purely expressive technique where the word "virtuosity" is an anomaly.

The work demands of the pianist, during the forty-minute duration, not only the greatest technique, but above all the comprehension of the state of mind and spirit that inspired the composer. We will proceed now to the analysis of this work.

* * *

Liszt, contrary to many other composers, in the first place did not describe his own feelings; he guided us toward heights from which one

[39] One hardly finds a trace of theoretical studies of harmony or counterpoint in his years of preliminary work, which caused Schumann to remark that Liszt, after all (sic), did not know his job as composer. As if all theory did not come after the works!

contemplates the wide spaces that stretch out around our lives. He speaks to us of human life in all its breadth, and even if he plunges us into meditation, one has the impression that these moments are only episodes. Those who expect to find in his music their personal thoughts, will comprehend neither the universal character, nor the epic aspect of this sonata.

The dominant factor in almost all of Liszt's compositions is his continuous rising above self.

From the beginning, the Sonata is not at all concerned with a matter of personal thoughts or sentiments. One recalls the Hebrew text of Genesis: "And the earth was without form and void; and darkness was upon the face of the deep." One finds in Creation, which continues to eternity, parallel evocations of solitude; there is in those landscapes something that pictures nature before man existed.

The first bars of this Sonata are a testimony of extra-human desolation. A Rumanian poet gives it this hallucinatory expression: "The sun is hidden behind the willows and the willows tremble to have hidden the sun."

At the beginning, three rests, long sustained, frame two *staccato* notes which are semi-abrupt but heavy, approaching the "*portato*." In order that the effect of the *pianissimo*, muffled and far distant, may not be lost, the damper pedal should be lifted simultaneously with the light and slow bounding of the hands so that the silence between is total. It must be deep, it must have been felt intensely by the performer, and this must be conveyed to the listener.

Then twice a descending scale with broken rhythm carries one to the abysmal depths of the lower notes. Liszt achieves his suspension of time in the first seven measures by three means: "*Lento assai*," "*Sotto voce*," and in sustaining with persistence the note G, during the whole of the descending scales. Reproduced below is the opening of the sonata:[40]

[40]The division of octaves between the hands, conforms to the oral tradition and is found only in rare editions.

exécution:

By holding very lightly on the G's, E flat, B flat of the first scale, on the G's, E flat, C sharp of the second scale, and in prolonging almost imperceptibly the interval after these notes, one obtains at the onset the rhythm that rules throughout the sonata.

After these seven (!) bars that seem an eternity, life surges with the swiftness of flame.

One rarely hears the octaves on the G's with the *éclat* that characterized the playing of a Busoni or Eugene d'Albert. Will this spark of life ever again burst forth in such a brilliant way?

Having thus received an inspiring breath of life, the Sonata soars. The following octaves should roll, from the 9th measure, in descending triplets and in ascending simple eighth notes, in an intersected burst, still hesitant, to end fifteen notes later in the deep register. If the opening bars plunge us into a *mood*, this melodic line traced in octaves immediately reveals the *design* of the work:

In consequence of the allusion made in the beginning of this chapter, we are firm in insisting on the distinction between *submitting to a mood* and *ascertaining the line of an action*. While admitting that, at the outset, one might still be mistaken in judging the state of mind or spirit of another because conveyed in a more or less hidden way by the expression on his face or in his eyes; on the contrary, one is all of a sudden enlightened as to the significance of the inner meaning of an action when it is profiled by a musical phrase. When the example cited above is placed next to the following that is found at the end of the Sonata:

what do we see?

By playing the theme at its first appearance (in octaves) quietly; the triplets without haste, preferably "*mezzo-staccato*"; the two ascents in simple eighth notes "*legatissimo*"; by terminating the descent with support and persistence; this alternating line between the treble and the bass recalls that line which a man's life traces when the history of his downfalls and his recoveries is revealed and brought to completion.[41]

If such a translation can in itself be judged arbitrary, the transformation of the theme at the end of the Sonata, which appears in the second example, reveals the solid foundation of this interpretation. The initial thought, the heroic opening, fades during the last repetition like a faraway memory. "Allegro energico" becomes "Adagio molto"; the descending triplets become simple eighth notes; the "*mezzo staccati*" become "*portati*." The same intervals are more slurred and lose themselves thus in our inner world with our most intimate thoughts in a final disengagement from the present. The evanescent phrase becomes one instant an interrogation, and a short funeral march on the G sharp, G natural; then, F sharp concludes this moving recall of the opening of the Sonata. In citing these two examples, our desire was to demonstrate how much a comparison agrees with and verifies musical thoughts.

[41]Shakespeare defines an accomplishment by the following succession: *to say, to do and to perform*, [English in the original].

Allowing for a certain amount of preconception in the idea suggested by a musical design, we have tried to give an extra musical demonstration which is nevertheless well related to an active or passive phenomenon. Let this example be a testimony of the equality between precision of mood and design. Here the identical harmonies interpret the same state of emotion.

Chopin,
Marche funèbre

Wagner,
Tristan, 3e acte

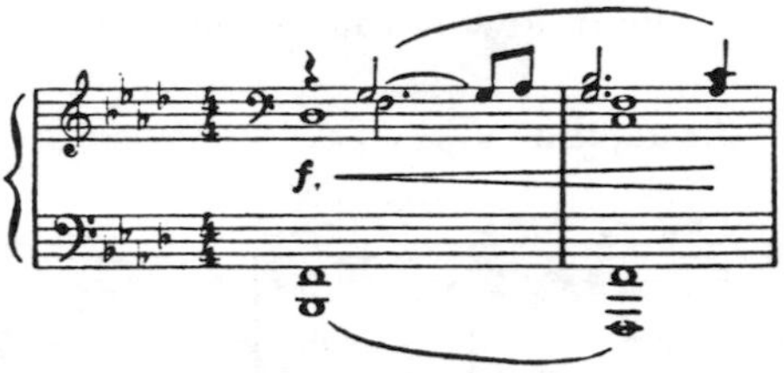

At the 13th measure the principal theme of the Sonata appears. This phrase, of a sober and heroic character, harmonized with a richness that one finds but rarely in musical literature, neatly characterizes Liszt in his second period of creation.

It is the general effect of theme and the accompaniment that we will examine. Let us separate the two staffs and study first the left hand. If one reflects that only four years separate this work from his Concerto in E flat, it is astonishing to see what changes occur in Liszt during this interim, how he translates his concept of heroism in these two works.

The opening of the earlier Concerto, given below, is a spontaneous leap of joy and of grandeur without the least presumption:

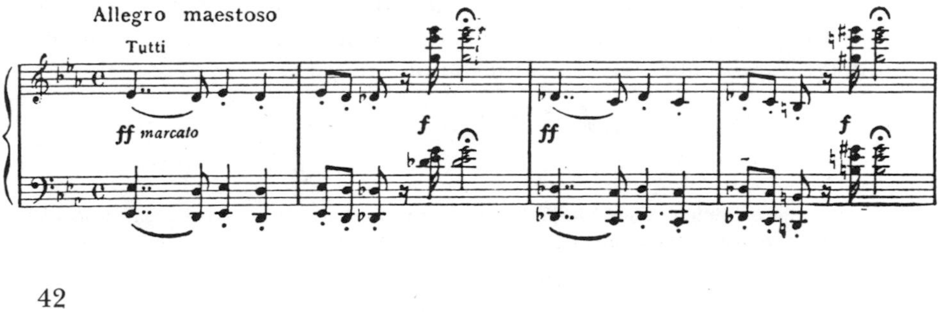

Quite different is the principal theme in the B minor Sonata, which is heard again and again during the episodes of the work, voiced with the same intervals, but with different rhythm. Without counting the near repetitions, one finds it nineteen times (in measures 13, 30, 141, 153, 171, 255, 310, 319, 349, 433, 465, 474, 484, 501, 506, 531, 616, 650 and 729).

In order to realize to what extent this phrase is totally transformed, measures 13 and 153 are a good illustration:

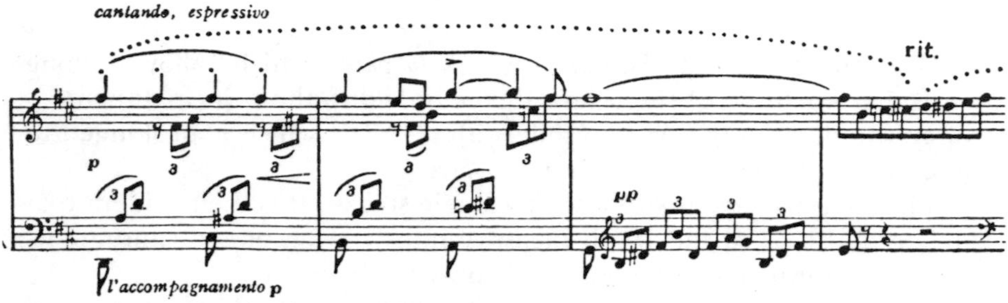

Far from being at the beginning a joyous burst, this phrase shows already—as was frequent in the first phrases of ancient tragedy—inexorable fate coming to pass. Only, above this expose of Liszt hovers another spirit that is lacking in the tragedies of the ancients: the consoling light. The same appears in certain pictures of the primitives where one sees angels who carry thorns and tears up to heaven. César Franck, the mystic, was rightly inspired by these measures in his *Variations symphoniques* . . .

Returning to the 13th measure, development of the three voices that the right hand plays merits attention. The top voice is a kind of adaptation of the octave theme, expressing an infinite tenderness that watches over the events of this world. This beatitude reappears in many places in the Sonata. Here we see Liszt on the luminous road to which we have alluded above, this path dominating the two others.

We stress the interpretation of what is written for the right hand: the *crescendo* in the 15th measure is misleading for those who are less familiar with the writing of Liszt. Yet, the picture of all his playing is delineated there. The *crescendo* is meant for the G and not for the A sharp, which would then falsely indicate the A sharp as a phrasing toward the *staccato* C sharp. The latter comes out of the D, and not at all from the A sharp.[42]

[42]Liszt would never tolerate gross accentuation of a passing note.

"But," one asks, "a *crescendo* on the G"? Certainly, we respond affirmatively, for there precisely is found the secret of the sonority prolonged and . . . increasing. In order to quiet the slightest doubt, we give a striking example of this possibility. Liszt wrote in "*l'Orage*" of *Pèlerinage en Suisse*[43] this:

Continuing with the Sonata, the *agitato piano* which follows—along with the repetition of the octave theme linked to the principal theme—open the door to the first episode with *le trille*[44] which is prolonged to almost the very end of the 113th measure.

This long passage is swept with a single stroke. It is then evident that the "grandioso" of the 105th measure must not become a tumultuous public demonstration of a bombastic bravura.[45]

From the structural point of view, the first episode shows a group of developments of themes, which must be why Liszt gave the name of "Sonata" to a work that is in reality a symphonic poem. The developments (*Durchführung*) of a structure so astonishing could one day arouse in the coldest mathematician the question: "And if, in spite of everything, intuition surpasses the most arduous calculations?" As none has ever charged Liszt with a mathematical construction of a composition [see fn. no. 39 p. 38] it is better to rely on the testimony of his intuition. One finds at the 51st measure, in the right hand, the astonishing phrasing of A to B sharp, from C sharp to D, from E sharp to F sharp, which causes the motif of octaves to burst forth, constituting with the chords in the left hand a harmonic march of perfect chords. Calculation? . . . We would really like to see this logarithmic machine!

At measure 120 begins the second episode that extends up to the *recitativo*. An organ-point on the chord A sharp, G, C sharp, E, G, E, has just brought the first to a conclusion and allows a totally new direction to be sensed.

[43]Eugene d'Albert insists particularly on this version in his Edition Bote and Bock, Berlin.

[44]*Le trille* is partially taken up by the right hand.

[45]All the pianists of Liszt's era played *allargando* in order to reduce the accumulated mass of sound, and thus the transparence remained intact.

To be noticed first in the new period of 85 measures beginning at the 120th, is that not one *forte* is to be found. To the peaceful reprise of the theme in octaves, reduced to one voice, are linked 16 measures "*dolce con grazia*" of infinite tenderness, enveloped in the slow grace-notes. With that return to the initial note, Liszt translates for the first time in the music, the idealization of a sentiment carried by the flight of thought. One finds there not only an exaltation of a sentiment but, even more, the clarity of inspiration.

Liszt was a fervent admirer of Dante, whose genius recognized as inherent to the proper meaning of paradise: the transcendent love of all things.

Still, the inspired musician does not compose *terzines* woven of sunbeams, without a single cloud. The questioning rests that characterize the music about which we speak are the poignant testimony:

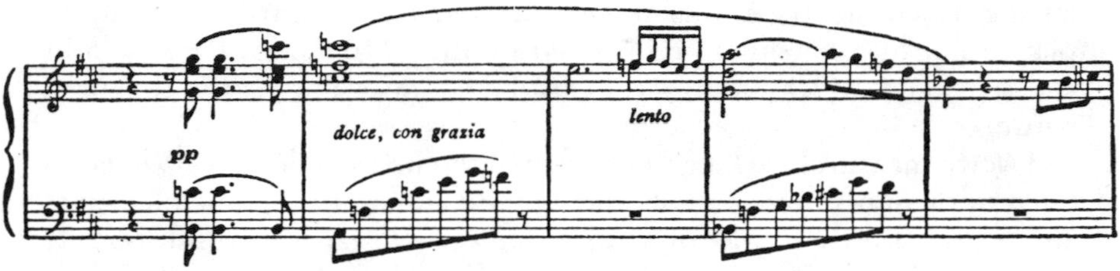

Considering this confusing complexity, one thinks of a painter who, for all time, elevated the clear-obscure into the domain of spirituality. We refer to Rembrandt and one of his greatest works: *La Famille*.[46]

The man in the middle distance, standing majestically in full consciousness of his destiny, seems charged with all of the cares that the happy group before him might encounter.

To draw forth beauty from a serious and heroic life is, as Rosenthal said of Liszt, "to see things with the eyes of a creator."

The Sonata is pursued by renewing the opening theme, now one of lyric quality. The intervals and notes remain the same; only the lengthening of their duration and the slow declamation accomplish this miracle.

Occasionally, some will not notice that the triplets of the 153rd measure played by the left hand, this time "*dolcissimo,*" hide the inversion of the octave theme. Here is a counterpoint that is not constructed by *aligned notation*, but by the *alignment of ideas* that are intertwined. In order to hear the relation between the harmonies, it should be emphasized that in the 167th measure (and other analogous measures), the last B sharp

---

[46]Brunswick Museum.

in the left hand, if one accents it lightly, goes toward the F sharp of the following chord in the right hand.

The elfish variations continue up to the trill (*dolce*) of the 197th measure, a trill evaporating playfully in a burst of grace-notes where one finds again the initial theme of octaves.

Suddenly, in the 205th measure, the tone of the epic is taken up again by an *agitato* through the 208th measure; and subsequently one hears the bewitching crystalline sounds that Schubert hid in his lied *Le roi des Aulnes*, when the latter whispers into the ear of the child: *Schöne Spiele spiel'ich mit dir*. The phrases of a great violence "*ff con strepito*" (measure 264) lead to a *tremolando*, cut by *fff* chords diminishing in the second and third chord like an alarming echo. The scales from the beginning of the Sonata descend like a menace and the theme of octaves, in "*staccato*," and in *fff* chords sustained by the pedal which is suddenly lifted rigorously and simultaneously with the last *staccato* chord, leaving the emptiness of an anguished silence. At this moment the *recitativo* is heard, not contemplative but of a harshness reinforced by the dissonance of E sharp in the left hand which, contrary to tradition, does not resolve in an E natural.

Twelve measures further the principal theme becomes a "*desperato*," a burst of the most violent revolt that exhausts itself during nine measures and evolves slowly by way of a *ritardando molto* towards its resolution. It becomes calm and transforms itself little by little in a hesitant *rallentando*. Then the "*ritardando molto*" leads to the Lento of three *pianissimo* chords. In this Adagio, the ensuing silence seems to enter the outside-of-time (measure 328). These measures introduce a contemplation of transcendent inspiration that only rare humans can know. This reversed circle of reflection (*repli sur soi-même*) reveals Liszt's soul in all its beauty. One can find this splendor in certain pages of the great mystics. Penetrating into the mystery of the Supreme Contemplation, Dante in "Paradise" of The Divine Comedy, notes the inexpressible when at the seventh *terzina* before the end he cries: "Oh Eternal Light which alone resides in you, which only you understand, and understood by you and understanding you, loves you and smiles upon you!"[47]

[47]Alexander Masseron. French translation of *La Divine Comédie*. Albin Michel, Paris, 1948-50.

Below is the passage just referred to:

Then is announced by broken arpeggios "*una voce, quasi adagio*," the beautiful Nocturne. The night is high and silent and covers with its immense vault the drama that played in a being at once anguished and full of wonder. One finds only in Chopin the same irresistible insistence, the same languor as in this poem, where only the ecstasy of melody changes the mood.

The Nocturne with two measures of entry:

Liszt never again found this incandescent tone of human love. In a later work, *La paraphrase de Méphisto*, the tone is more bleak, more morbid from the beginning, even to the last measures where Faust flees the suffocating atmosphere and finds release in nature, in the bright clear morning that evokes the long trills of birds. In comparing these two pieces of music, one can meditate on the difference between divine voluptuousness and sheer sensuality, which is after all, voluptuousness distorted, made material. Plato's words on this subject thunder, as coming from the universe: "There are two sorts of ecstasy, one being the exaltation of divine forces, the other being human weakness."

Returning to the Sonata, the Nocturne is linked to several pages of frenzied agitation, a recital of unchained passion which only inspiration of a higher order can halt. Witness then, the recovery that can be made only by powers residing in the roots of a being who has long cultivated them. This control is expressed in the measures which follow, resembling those of the Andante sostenuto where despair is calmed. The ensuing

series of wandering scales lead to the Fugue, which is nothing other than a representation of the triumph of reason. The entire Fugue is a restatement of the Sonata, clearer and more objective.

A veritable explosion of expressive power ends abruptly after measure 554. Apocalyptic falls, first to the bass chord of E flat major, then to E minor in the deep depths. In this tableau it is from the enormous height of four octaves that one hangs over the implacable descent of the initial scale motif, which this time thunders in the middle of hallucinatory echoes. It is a vision of the Last Judgment, and at the same time during this grandiose and terrible scene, above it all reigns a spirit perfectly calm; as if an observer, sure of safe-keeping, described with the pen of a St. John the most upsetting of spectacles.

In these pages the cosmic awareness of Liszt takes complete form. But it is only with difficulty that one concedes to music a quality which primitive painters have already shown us for centuries.

Surrealism is as ancient as the world, less profound, but infinitely more encompassing than abstract art; it represents the universal idea that hovers above the existence of man and of the world. When one studies the primitives and later Tintoretto and El Greco, the superposition of celestial and terrestrial scenes, one understands the justness of this simultaneity. Their realism, exalted by the profound conviction of their belief, induces them to break the barrage of frontiers between the real and the unreal. This obliteration of frontiers is not so improbable, since in daily living one makes this adjustment every moment. Does it not take a great deal of forgetfulness to silently tolerate the incompatibility of everyday acts with the aspirations? If man desires to contemplate his life from on high and only in its grand outlines, it furnishes salvation from the view of small humans whose horizons are too narrow.

In this sense, but very much more powerfully, the artist creates his work. This detachment from the real and this aiming toward the unreal made Liszt create pages such as we have spoken of.

In the 554th measure is accomplished the most universal of detachments. Aside from the apocalyptical scenes, one hears in the 600th measure the triumphant song of trumpets accompanied by peals of bell-ringing; one hears the reminiscence of joys and terrestrial illusions in measures 609-615. The lyric theme has become a far away memory, and in the 634th measure one "hears rise from the ship—Oh Rimbaud—the song of angels."

What a display of contrasts! It is in the 673rd measure that one thinks for a moment that the composer allows Liszt to exceed himself by the power of his pen. But no, the joy which bursts is as vibrant as the beauty of this turbulence of octaves. There is absolutely no presumption in their flight, the ascending and descending line is this time without interruption,

the left hand replenishing the rests. It is not the empty demonstration of a trickery of octaves that is necessary here; it is the large flight toward space. It is the last testimony of the full and illustrious splendor of terrestrial events, that tremble like the joy of a *Te Deum* rising from crowds in ecstasy.

The Andante sostenuto brings us finally to the inmost recess of Liszt's heart when he reviews the events of his life with the gratitude of someone who sees it in retrospect before taking his last road.

In the 32nd measure before the end, the theme, indicated "*portato*," with two "*staccato*" notes before each repetition, sounds the knell on the noble and heroic life.

The chords in the right hand slowly ascend toward one that is luminous; from that point the metamorphosis takes place:

The epic draws to its close and fades little by little in the spirit of the hero whose soul separates itself upon entering eternity. We give again

these few measures and entreat our readers to study and meditate this writing:

The *portato*, hesitant, on the D sharp, E, F sharp is followed by a slow descent, progressively slower, down to the A.

Do we not hear in the character of these three *portato adagio* notes, almost imperceptible, a weakened voice that inquiries before the final surrender "Where am I . . .?"

After the brief funeral march, two chords broken by longer and longer silences introduce the Lento assai.

In this very poignant ending, the scale of the opening of the Sonata proceeds towards five chords of an ineffable beauty. Each of these chords is placed on the fourth beat of the measure. Listening to these diaphanous sonorities, thought may travel beyond and recall the last vision of the Apocalypse:

"And there shall be no night there; and they shall need nor the light of a lamp, nor the light of the sun, for the Lord God giveth them light . . ."

One lone note "*staccato pianissimo*" in the very low bass concludes this work, putting a last accent on the life of this world already far away.

PART II: THE BIRTH OF A METHOD

Introduction to Chapter Four

"Only divine love grants the keys to science."[48]

We pause ahead of subject matter, which is for the most part purely technical, to consider the question that certain pianists ask: "Doesn't that sort of knowledge acquired by studying profoundly the act of playing destroy intuitive execution?"

The contrary is our firm conviction. Although intuition may be a knowledge of those truths that do not need reasoning for an intermediary in order to be grasped by the mind, their intellectual confirmation acts as a new stimulation towards new intuitions. It is often forgotten that when intuition manifests itself in the domain of technique, it is intimately bound to former experiences. No one can just sit down and play an instrument without some previous acquaintance with it.

What other reason could there be for not following this evolution but fear of knowing oneself and of becoming conscious of one's acts? Without realizing it, the opponents of conscious technique are acting against their own aspirations. Isn't the very essence of their belief in intuition that it opens new horizons to their ideals?

All aim for perfect interpretation. With such a goal, it is imperative to know the secrets of the act of playing in order to be able to attain perfection in technique, which in turn constitutes the primary condition for the interpretation of our masterworks.

Liszt was a model of this: "In the course of my life I was always forced to do all this by instinct to begin with, and then more and more consciously with time." *(Ich habe das alles stets im Leben zunächst instinktiv, dann immer mehr und mehr bewuszt ausüben müssen.)*[49]

The research for our books preceding this one[50] was done according to these principles. The first statements concerning bounce and of rebound in the works of Liszt and Chopin were not our invention, but simply the revelation of a fact. Our only merit was to accept what did not come from ourself. In the first of these works one can follow the development from the initial fact discovered, beginning at the point of departure which was revealed thanks to a lucky discovery in Liszt's writing. During this development we have not allowed ourself to reject any consequences into which we have been led. The *exposé* of this discovery

---

[48] J. Arthur Rimbaud, A Season in Hell. *La Mercure de France,* Paris, 1914.

[49] F. H. Clark, op cit., page 60.

[50] See Appendix C for complete list of musical and literary works of Paul Roës.

and of our subsequent research happened in the following order: first the discovery of the bounce, which appears to us as a natural consequence of the powerful properties of the flexors[51] and of the action of those muscles under the influence of the weight of the arm; next, the possibility of the lightening of the arm by forces which each one of us possesses; then the manifestation of the power of pronation,[52a] which appeared to us at first as only partially evident, as one can see on page 13 of *L'Elément fondamental.* This new phenomenon assumed a greater significance two years later, in the fifth chapter of *La Musique et l'Artisan,* through the study of gyratory movements, a significance brought into full light only at the present moment.

During twenty years of experience, it has been given to us to realize what at one time we only sensed, and what we will explain in the chapter which follows: "The Birth of a Method."

[51]See alphabetical nomenclature, (page 58.)

[52a]Id. (page 59.)

Alphabetical Nomenclature

Abduction	Movement which takes a limb away from the axis of the body.
Adduction	Movement which approaches a limb toward the axis of the body.
Axis of the Body	Imaginary vertical line down the center of the body. [plumb line]
Brachial Apparatus	The whole ensemble of arm and shoulder.
Bringing the arm inside	Movement which carries the arm toward the center of the body, and goes beyond the body if the movement is of great amplitude.
Carpal Canals	Canals in the form of pipes enveloping the tendons, or chords uniting the fingers and wrist, and running through the palm of the hand.
Development	Equivalent of "contraction," but which we prefer because the word contraction is often wrongly taken as a synonym for crispation, for stiffness. We use the word "development" to designate a light muscular contraction.
Eminence, Thenar	The salient part underneath the hand which is formed by the motor muscles of the thumb; both those which fold the thumb under the palm, and those which open the thumb out away from the palm.
Eminence, Hypo-thenar	The salient part underneath the hand containing notably the flexor muscle which folds the fifth finger under the palm.
En dedans [Inside]	The top part turned towards the body, the under side towards the exterior (speaking of the position of the hand or of the arm), while moving towards the body (if a movement is involved).
En dehors [Outside]	The top part turned towards the exterior, the under side towards the body (position of the hand or of the arm), while moving away from the body (when referring to a movement).

Extensors .... Muscles which extend or raise the fingers. Muscles which, bending the wrist, raise the hand towards the back, toward the top of the forearm.

Flexors .... Muscles which fold the fingers. Muscles which lower the hand [clench the fist].

Free fall .... We do not, of course, use this term in the meaning which it has in physics, which is not suitable to the fall of the arm articulated at the shoulder. The term "free fall," much used in the language of piano technique, means: the fall, down to the bottom of the key, of the mass of the extended arm, *liberated from all constraint* (fear, contraction of the muscles of the shoulder or of the back, spasmodic curling up of the hand), consequently, *in a total letting go.*

Free weight .... The principle of "free weight" differs from that of "free fall" (see this word) in that the finger is already on the key, immobile, while an instantaneous and total relaxation of the dorsal muscles which support the extended arm liberates the arm. In spite of the absence of acquired speed (contrary to the case of the free fall), the key is powerfully depressed by the finger which is going to find support on the bottom of the key, for serving as a pillar or for a rebound.

Inside .... See *en dedans.*

Intercalated (note) ..... A little anchor note played by the fifth finger, inserted between each note of a musical passage studied, in order to facilitate the motion of pronation. Later on, this supporting note assumes only an imaginary existence.

Inter-ossial (muscles) ... Small muscles of the fingers having diverse motor functions, situated between the bones of the palm of the hand (metacarpals).

Ligaments .... Bands of strong, fibrous tissue which connect bones.

Outside .... See *en dehors.*

Pronation	Rotation of the hand inwards, making the thumb turn downward. Rotation inwards of the arm.
Supination	The inverse movement from that of pronation, that is to say, rotation of the hand outwards, turning the fifth finger downwards.
Tendon	A tough cord or band of inelastic fibrous tissue connecting the fleshy part of a muscle to a bone, muscle, or organ of the body.
Triceps	The three-headed extensor muscle along the back of the upper arm, serving, relative to reference here, to extend the forearms.
Vault with a high arch .	The form which the hand assumes when, the fingers taking support on the depressed keys, the back of the hand moves upwards while the "crux" of the palm of the hand deepens on the under side. [In Paul Roës' earlier book, *Essai sur la Technique du Piano,* he likens this vault to crossed croquet wickets.]

CHAPTER FOUR

The Reconstitution of Liszt's Playing: The Method

I.

Our daily experience has given to all of us the notion of weight, as well as that of the accelerated drop of a falling body.

Let us remember that the weight of a body is the measure of the force, proportionate to its mass, which is exercised on that body by the gravity which draws it towards the center of the earth; the tiny variations of this weight depending on latitude and altitude, are quite negligible with regard to our purposes here. Let us also recall that in all places the direction in which weight acts, the "vertical" of that place, is indicated by the plumb line. And that without the resistance to their fall which the air furnishes, all bodies, whatever their density or their form, when let go from the same height in a given place, would fall with the same speed, uniformly accelerated. In the vacuum of Newton's classic glass tube, grains of lead and bird feathers fall in the same way.

First Experiment

A rubber ball, when released from above a table, falls and rebounds vertically. At the instant of the shock the ball flattens a little, but almost immediately through an instant reaction due to its elasticity and which restores to it its form, its substance acts as a spring which, taking as fulcrum the resistant surface of the table, throws the ball back in the opposite direction from its fall, thus restoring the work absorbed in its deformation. Here is an example of "elastic shock": without the inevitable losses of energy inherent in the nature of things, the quantity of energy acquired by the ball from the fact of its elevation above the table would conserve itself completely and the ball, progressively slowed down by gravity, would bounce up to its initial level; a new fall would follow, and so on indefinitely. Because of the renewed losses however, the movement dies out rapidly, the ball rebounding only a certain number of times, lower and lower as the energy becomes dissipated.

Second Experiment

When, instead of letting the ball fall vertically, one throws it parallel or obliquely to the table, the trajectory, under the influence of gravity, becomes curved, following a parabolic arc which conducts the ball to a

first point of rebound. The ball rebounds several times, as in the preceding experiment, but follows a parabolic trajectory between two successive points of fall, and in each of these the angle of reflexion is equal to the angle of incidence. The movement dies as before, on account of the gradual loss of the energy which was set in motion.

We shall see how the results of these experiments can be transposed into piano playing when taking into account the constitution of the human body.

II.

The Table of Playing

Just as the piano possesses a table of harmony, a table of resonance which reflects the vibrations of the strings, it also contains a table of rebound, which reflects *the action* of the pianist. It is found beneath the row of keys. It arrests further depression of the keys, a solid base on which the action of the bounce is established. The quality, the firmness of this base, is of primary importance for this way of playing.

The pianos are often inadequate because of the softness of the felt discs used as cushions. This bottom onto which the keys descend, too often resembles the ground in the swamps where the walker searches in vain for firm earth. Unevenness at the bottom of the keyboard is prejudicial to the free bounce. In order that the possibility of an adequate bounce may be assured, the felt discs must be firm. Their capacity for compression must be a half millimeter.[52b] It is to this height that a key must recover, while the weight of the arm and of the hand, through the intervention of the back muscles, will be almost totally withheld, so that only the weight of the fingers is keeping the key down. It goes without saying that the depth of the depression of the key will not go beyond the normal distance, nor will it be too weak.

III.

Before proceeding to the application of our two experiments to piano playing, we state two necessary conditions for good success.

First: It is indispensable to have a natural and easy gesture at the keyboard. This gift, necessary for becoming a good pianist, is more often lacking in the students than is their musical understanding; in a perfect

---

[52b]*Ed. note:* A half millimeter amounts to approximately .02 of an inch. Keep in mind, throughout all such future references in the book, that a centimeter equals .3937 of an inch; a millimeter equals .03937 of an inch.

equilibrium of the performance these gifts complement each other harmoniously.

One can acquire beautiful and subtle motions through the music itself, but the supple gesture is rarely inborn, accomplished without contraction, without useless exaggerations, and free from extraneous motions. In order to acquire it, the pianist must necessarily also encounter it outside of his occupation. The beautiful supple gesture "borrowed from space" allows "breathing" of the muscle, which is as vital as the respiration of our lungs. The necessary adaptation must therefore be attempted with that unconcern, that ease which is the contrary of the painful apprehension which can be observed in those who feel selfconscious about their heavy and angular movements. Generosity and grandeur are necessary for understanding an action.

Second: The pianist must sit at a height which allows him to feel the weight of the arm in its entirety. If the chair is too high, the arm hangs down nearly vertically. Here there is no possibility of "free fall"[53] in playing. The arm feels its own weight more when it is held horizontally. Chopin instructs us on this subject; he used to lean backwards and in this position he favored keeping the elbow almost totally extended at the height of the white keys.

Let us observe this subtle distinction between the height of the white keys and that of the black keys. While leaning lightly towards the rear, Chopin's arms were in an almost horizontal position. The number of great pianists using a low seat is considerable. After studying Liszt's position at the piano in the previous chapter, we might now add the names of Paderewski, Teresa Carreño, Siloti, Godowsky and Elly Ney, who sat very low.

The theorists who lived during the great epoch of the nineteenth century, such as Leschetizky and later, Deppe, adopted the low position. Many a contemporary virtuoso having adopted the high position "slugs" and hammers from a great height, even when leaning way forward, and all one hears are noises and groans on the keys and in the strings. And this is not astonishing, if one considers that insufficiency of weight must be compensated for by an effort. This manner of playing is quite spectacular, but has no relationship whatever to the kind of playing which draws miracles from our well-nigh mysterious instrument.

Let us study now in what way the constitution of the human body lends itself to the adaptation of our two experiments to piano playing.

To the first experiment, we give two different aspects of this process: (1) the bouncing of the mass of the arm and of the hand after an *unin-*

---

[53]In order to avoid all misunderstanding concerning the meaning of the term "free," we beg the reader to read the definition which is given in the nomenclature, (p. 58.)

terrupted fall towards the bottom of the keys; (2) the bouncing of this mass after a fall *interrupted* at the moment when the falling mass approaches the keys but continued, after that, to the bottom of its trajectory for another ten millimeters.

If below, we refer to the terms: "to drop" or "to fall," it is for the purpose of explaining a theoretical action. In actual playing, these terms no longer have the same meaning.

First Aspect:

Seated at the piano, low enough to permit maximum use of the weight of the arm, that is to say, the arm stretched out horizontally, let this mass fall from a height of thirty centimeters above the keyboard onto one or several keys, with no holding it back. Take care that the fingers are lightly rounded. The shock will be brutal and the sound consequently very harsh. To keep the hand from sliding onto the knees, one will tighten the tendons[54] and the muscles at the moment of stopping.

This light development[55] of the muscles is accomplished instinctively. Scarcely in contact with the ivory, the fingertips have a tendency to cling to it, provided however, that the distance between the pianist and his instrument is sufficiently great. If the fingers cling thus to the keys (adherence of the fingers), the hand will not slide off the keyboard.

It is through the adherence of the fingers, the tension of the tendons, and the development of the flexors,[56] that the stretched-out arm in its full length, resembles a *"suspension bridge" between two points of support:* the finger and the shoulder joint. The lowest point in this bridge will be the wrist, then the elbow. The triceps[57] take no part in this formation of the suspended bridge; they are only used to stretch out the arm before the fall. Once the bridge is established, one immediately feels the possibility of a spring in the fingers, running up into the palm of the hand, the wrist, and the underside of the forearm. At first this spring, in spite of its elasticity, will not have enough power to throw the hand and arm back up above key level. In order to effect this rebound another force must intervene. This force is situated in the musculature of the back and in that of the shoulder. These are the muscles which raise the arm up in front (up to the vertical), from a relaxed position hanging down alongside the body. These groups of muscles therefore can *raise* the arm as well as *support* it. This *dosage* in their functioning is of primary impor-

[54]See nomenclature, (page 59.)

[55]Id. (page 57.)

[56]Id. (page 58.)

[57]Id. (page 59.)

tance for the action of bouncing and for that which continues it: the rebound.

We present a short outline of the stages of the bouncing; in other words, a review of its course:

a. At the moment of the shock, a suspension bridge is formed. It is held in equilibrium by the adherence of the fingers, the tension of the tendons, and the development of the flexors.

b. At the same instant, this bridge yields a little bit and the wrist drops slightly below the keyboard without, however, touching it.

c. Under the constant weight of the arm which is still outstretched, the spring, which had just yielded, now tightens again while the wrist and the forearm go down, and will be tensed more strongly than before.

d. The spring, under the accumulated tension, then immediately gives the signal to the musculature of the arm and shoulder to lighten the weight.

One can facilitate the execution of the whole of the four phases, *a, b, c* and *d,* by dividing it into two phases only. One group, *a* and *b,* into one movement and after that one executes *c* and *d,* likewise combined into one gesture. By means of this combined action, hand and arm are trajected above the level of the keys.

This upward thrust of the whole organism of the arm, of the forearm, and of the hand is performed therefore without the finger being raised by its extensor, without the hand being raised by the wrist, without these organs being raised by the forearm, but the whole ensemble of these organs and of the outstretched arm will be pushed up by the contraction of the spring which is found in the palm of the hand, in the finger, and on the underside of the forearm, an infinitesimal fraction of a second after the lightening of the whole organism by the power of the shoulder and of the back.

It is indeed an explosive movement directed from low to high, seconded by the intervention, minutely dosed, of the elevating power which resides in the back and in the shoulder.

Second Aspect:

From the vertical fall there results a bounce which is equally vertical.

The bird, following a dizzying descent, places himself lightly on the ground. He accomplishes this by spreading out his wings just before he lands. He thus makes a cushion of air which protects him against too brutal a shock. We compare this manner of descent and landing with the free fall of the outstretched arm toward the keyboard, when the falling mass is suddenly arrested almost at key level through the intervention of the portative and elevative forces residing in the back and

the shoulder. What the deployment of the bird's wings supplies to prevent a killing shock, so does the intervention of the powerful muscles of the back and shoulder arrest the fall of the arm.

This comparison should be considered merely in a suggestive sense. The bird creates a resisting force which opposes his fall, by means of the "cushion of air" supplied by spreading his wings; however it is an acting force, one that resides in the musculature of the back, which arrests the fall of the arm.

There is a potential of gravitation remaining just as the fingers reach the surface of the keys. One realizes this by feeling the weight of the arm as if it were suddenly suspended at the shoulder. This weighing mass, if the sitting position is low, possesses sufficient energy to depress the keys with considerable power even though the distance down to the bottom of the key is very short.

Thus, for the principle of "free fall," that of "free weight" may be substituted. By relaxing the contraction of the back and the shoulder, the fall continues and the key this time, is pressed down. For a brief instant, as we have seen in the account of the interrupted fall, the arm will resume the position of suspended bridge and the maneuver of the bounce then occurs [as described in the First Aspect]. The sound will be of great intensity, round and mellow; one will hear a resonant "nucleus" corresponding marvelously to *energy produced at the moment and at the point desired.* The rebound which succeeds this initial easily controlled depression of the keys, *millimeter by millimeter,* will be in its turn extremely differentiated.

By the use of natural forces, and within the ensemble of only vertical movements, the pianist already has possession of a means which the technique of raising the fingers cannot give him. Notice also that during this light rebound the fingers themselves, being for a moment inert, do not lose contact with the ivory. The hand will control the development[58] of the arm. However, the dosage of the forces used will determine the amplitude of the rebound. This maneuver of contractions can be repeated indefinitely without fatigue, thanks to (and uniquely because of) the presence of the table of playing from which all the action of piano playing takes life.

In summary, we see that every movement of bouncing, and consequently of rebounding [bouncing off], is defined by: a balance between the forces of nature on the one hand, and the muscular forces on the other.

[58]See nomenclature, (page 57.)

A study of the adaptation of our second physical experiment, that of the rebound in the lateral sense, is the next consideration.

Taking inspiration from the example of a ball given above, one lets the extended arm fall obliquely in the direction of the axis[59] of the body, while trying to take support through one of the fingers on the bottom of a key. One is careful that the arm muscles are not contracted, but only in development [light contraction] and that the fingers are lightly curved.

As soon as it meets the table of playing the mass will be thrown over towards the side of the thumb. At the moment of launching this gesture on the bias simulates a lateral propulsion, that is to say parallel to the keyboard, but gravity immediately draws the impulse into a curved line. The starting movement in anatomical terms is called adduction, or "sending the arm inside."[60]

The pianist directs a considerable muscular force to this execution. During the curved descent this force stimulates a second action: inward turning of the arm and this rotation, reflected by the forearm, results in pronation[61] of the hand.

The maneuvers of rotation and of pronation, the first [stemming mostly from the ball and socket joint of the shoulder] actuating the second, cause the arm instinctively to curve (lightly), so that the elbow and the wrist are turned outside.[62] Conscious of these movements of rotation which are generated and of the pushing outwards of the elbow and of the wrist, the pianist resumes the maneuver.

What happens then?

The curve, formed by the elbow, the forearm and the wrist, will serve at the moment of impact, as a counterbalance. Immediately this counterbalance yields, and reestablishes the equilibrium of the hand which had been thrown over the thumb. It is to be noted that the triceps[63] plays only a very slight role during this action. For the moment, this lateral fall will not produce the formation of a suspended bridge in the true sense of the word; rather, as expressed by Chopin, the finger will serve as a pillar. By the light inclination of the hand towards the thumb, the adherence of the finger makes itself felt now in a lateral direction. In continuing the action, the bounce will effect itself in the same way as in the vertical bound. At first it seems, because of the deviation in an oblique

---

[59]See nomenclature (page 57.)

[60]Id. See "Bringing" the arm inside, (page 57.)

[61]Id. (page 59.)

[62]Id. (page 58.)

[63]Id. (page 59.)

direction, that a new spring enters into play. In reality, it is a reaction of the same flexor,[64] only that the inter-ossial[65] muscles intervene to attenuate the effect of the lateral leaning which is experienced by the joints of the finger taking part in the action.

In resume, we have just given a demonstration of two bounces, one in a vertical direction, the other in an oblique [or lateral-wise] direction.

We now give an example in which the two bounces comes into play. These measures are taken from Liszt's Sonata in B minor. It is the initial theme of the Fugue, and one finds there the original fingering.[66]

The fingering is authentic. This fingering is one of the first discoveries that gave the author of this book inspiration to reconstruct the composition of the playing of this most eminent pianist. Here are the measures in question:

We will study attentively the passing of the C to the D flat. According to the fingering, these two notes must be played with the same second finger and the execution is ultra-rapid. The first is a white key, a lower level key, the second, that of arrival, is a black key, a higher level key.

The first note is linked to the second; the latter is marked *staccato* as well as those which immediately follow. If one plays them by raising the fingers, the indicated *legato* will be interrupted. Furthermore, the space which the finger must travel is too great to strike the D flat on time. How to manage it? The bounce in an oblique direction when departing from the C is the only solution possible. Only the resistance from this depressed key will facilitate the liaison, by throwing the finger high enough to reach the D flat and furnish the impetus to continue the *staccato* on the following three D flats. Therefore, Liszt without question utilized the oblique [lateral] bounce; where the oblique or lateral bounce becomes an expedient device, the vertical bounce follows with ease.

This example fully reveals the phenomenon but does not yet account for its profound significance. One cannot at once foresee that the act of pronation which this example demonstrates will be recognized as the

---

[64]See nomenclature (page 58.)

[65]Id. (page 58.)

[66]The authenticity of this fingering is contested by certain pianists for reasons which are probably justified by their own particular technique. It is to be found, however, in the autograph and, above all, has been transmitted to this author by those disciplies of Liszt whom we have known personally. Among these are Emil von Sauer, Eugene d'Albert and Moriz Rosenthal.

prime factor in all execution of piano playing. The complete supremacy of pronation,[67] which minimizes the importance of supination,[68] was impossible to see at the first moment we realized that Liszt must have used this lateral bounce. Pronation applied on the fifth finger, which henceforth would serve as point of departure for pronation in the other four fingers, was still an unsuspected reality.

IV.

Among the innumerable photos of pianists' hands, that of Liszt generally represents a strange object of curiosity. Comments made by the reproducers of this photo reveal their astonishment with a hand that seems to them an enigma; so mysterious and completely different from others. First, one does not understand the position of the thumb almost completely hidden under the index finger. Except for this example of Liszt, an analogous but less evident phenomenon is found in the hand of Carl Tausig, as can be seen in a picture in possession of the heirs of Professor Klindworth. Eugene d'Albert's hand manifests in its expansion a pronounced tendency towards the folding under of the thumb. However, no other photo shows as ostensibly the thumb turned inwards, the phalange turned outside.[69] Reproduced here is L. Held's photo of the original cast which is in the Franz Liszt Museum in Weimar.

What first strikes the imagination in looking at this hand is its appearance. Here is a hand which gives the impression of rotating on its axis, and the direction of this movement is incontestably towards the thumb. This inclination towards pronation finds itself singularly reenforced by the position of the wrist which is clearly raised on the exterior side. As for the fifth finger, it is evident that the movement of supination is seriously hindered by the fact that the position of the thumb gets in the way of this outward rotation.

And the picture of Chopin's hand comes to our mind. The cast of this hand shows a fifth finger curved towards the inside. Supination towards, and on, this bent finger was practically impossible. It was useless. One knows his theory: that the fingers serve first of all as pillars. Now, in supination his curved fifth finger would have offered nothing but a mediocre possibility as a pillar of support. In the light of our second experiment the reader already catches a glimpse of what pronation supplies for the fifth finger alone. This movement which, as we have seen,

[67]See nomenclature (page 59.)

[68]Id. (page 59.)

[69]Id. (page 58.)

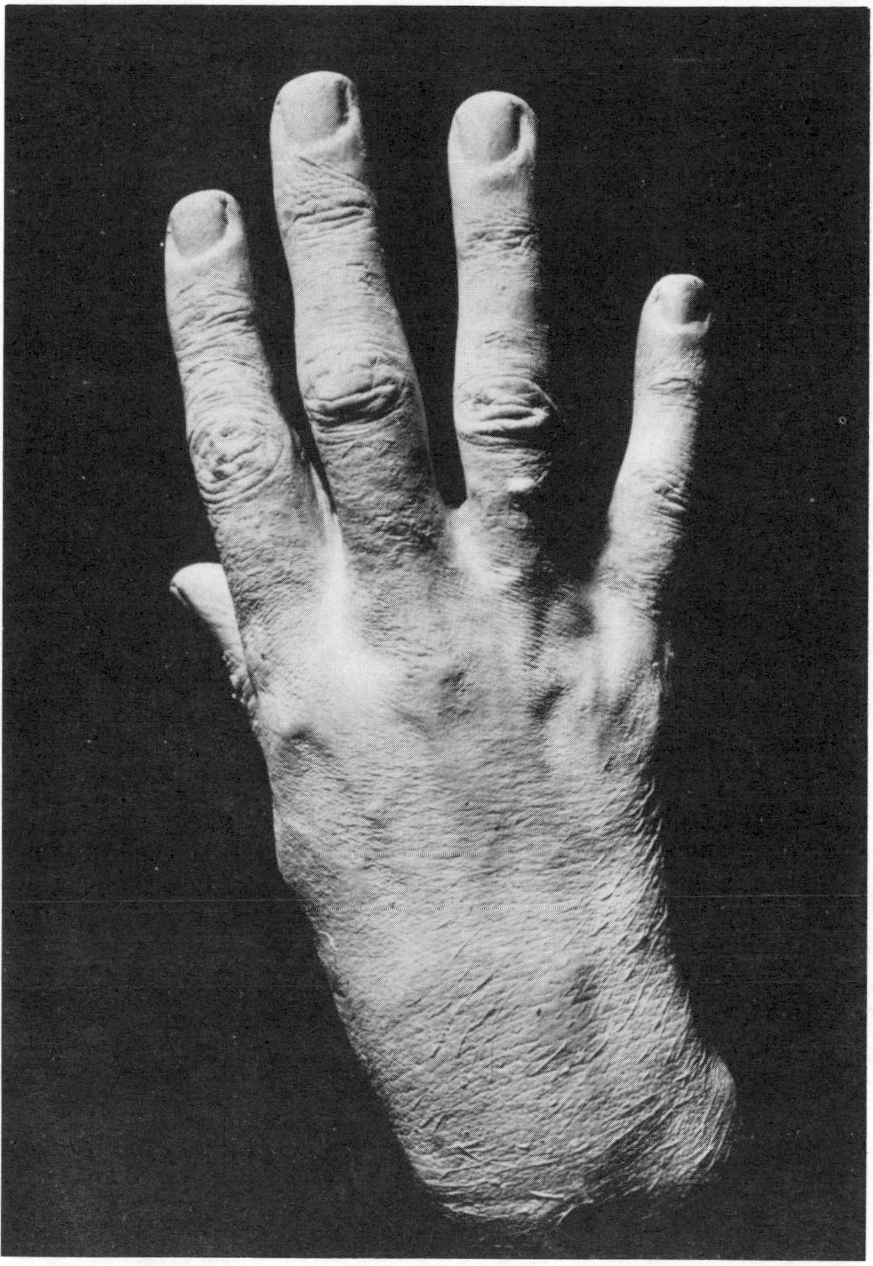

Photo L. Held

Cast of Franz Liszt's hand (Franz Liszt Museum)

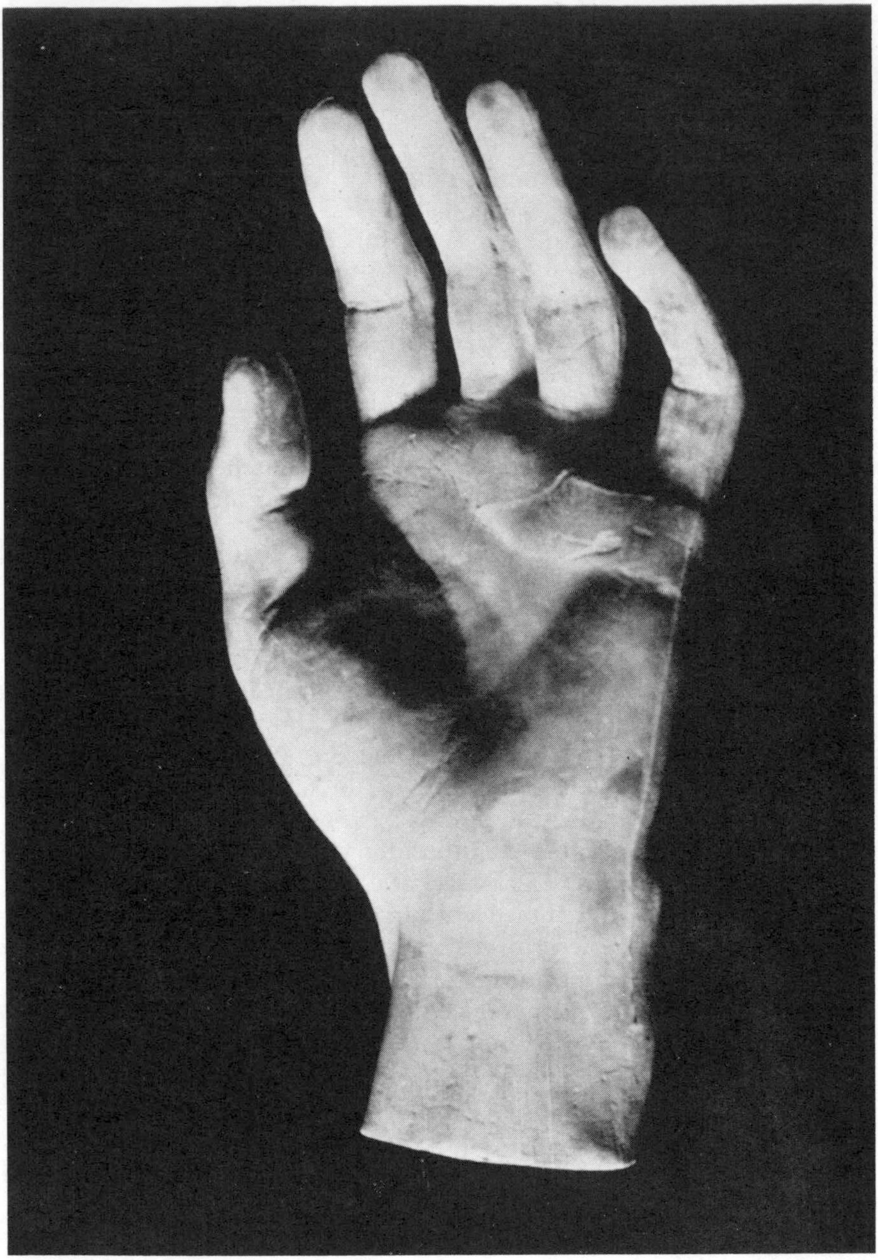

Photo J. Roubier

Cast of Frédéric Chopin's hand, made by Clésinger (Musée Carnavalet)

has its source in the back, the shoulder and the forearm, serves notably not only to position the little finger perpendicularly on the key, but also to allow it more easily to continue pronation.

Returning to the study of Liszt's hand, the placing inside[70] of the thumb is necessary for the freedom in playing of the other fingers. We have amply demonstrated the role of the flexors as the basis of our study. All we have said concerning free fall, free weight, table of playing, bounce and rebound, is centered on the power of the flexor muscles, those which depress the keys and which serve as active springs. The tendons of these muscles pass through the palm of the hand. They are surrounded by canals which are called the carpal canals.[71] These latter are in their turn surrounded by ligaments.[72] The folding movement of the thumb onto the palm of the hand is performed by the thenar eminence.[73] In thus folding the thumb one liberates the carpal canals from the light pressure of the fibres which surround them and consequently one renders a greater freedom to the functioning of the tendons on the inside of the canals.

The flexibility of the motion which depresses the keys is therefore greatly increased through the folding under of the thumb.

If one tests the experiment it is easy to prove by simply feeling the difference in flexibility on the inside of the hand. When one extends the thumb, the palm tightens; if one folds the thumb under, the palm loosens.

With this in mind the picture of Liszt's folded thumb changes character, as will be illustrated later on by studying the execution of the Third Paganini-Liszt Etude. This time it will be the hand, through the action of pronation, which covers the thumb. Liszt's ease of playing thus finds its apogee through the complete utilization of natural resources.

It is quite probable that Liszt never studied the anatomy of the hand, but it is certain that, guided by his prodigious clairvoyance and intuition, he found a technical execution without equal. It is Chopin rather, the meticulous searcher, constantly analyzing his movements, who would have been interested in this science. The ingenious technician who divided the octave into four minor thirds, who constructed the scale by placing the thumb on a white key and the two or three following fingers on the black keys, would have continued as well his research on the role of the fingers, up to anatomical analysis.

It is often the opinion that Chopin found his way through intuition and Liszt through intelligence, but the contrary was more often the case.

---

[70]See nomenclature (page 58.)

[71]Id. (page 57.)

[72]Id. (page 58.)

[73]Id. (page 57.)

V.

Let us now leave the anatomical domain. Expounding physical realities, infinitely less attractive than the domain of thought, has been necessary as a background for the method which one sees taking form little by little.

If from this beginning the light of an idea gleams forth, we rejoice over it.

Let us now make the bells ring in the Third Paganini-Liszt Etude, *la Campanella.* There are many who do not like this composition. But one too often finds among these, individuals whose evaluation confuses amusing levity with joyful lightness. A second reason for their aversion to this sparkling work is the inability to execute it with ease. Thus unfavorable criticism is sometimes the result of a lack of technical means.

For this study we use the Breitkopf and Härtel edition of 1899, which is a faithful reproduction of the autograph. After four measures of introduction, all *staccato* notes, one finds a series of these same sharp "*staccati*" played by the fifth finger of the right hand and played also by the chords of the left hand. What does it mean to play a *staccato* note? We take as an example of this execution the *pizzicati* of stringed instruments. First the fingertip grasps the string lightly, then lets it go by pulling it out. A similar gesture is possible at the piano. It is not superfluous to say that this movement is particularly stimulated by the imagination in order to be executed materially afterwards. This distinction between the two stages is useful for good execution. It will prevent the haste of wanting to pinch the key before contact with it. One sees clearly this gesture, delicate and affected, which wishes to make a "pretty" sound. The violinist, the cellist, and above all, the harpist avoid this parasitical movement. Their action will be firm and effective.

In transferring this action to the piano, one first makes contact with a key, then rejects it brusquely by bouncing still more suddenly, with a speed which corresponds to the need for either a short sound, or a relatively short one. Let us refer to our second adaptation, recalling the arrest prior to the act of depressing the key. This precept requires us to place the finger first, in order to depress the key afterwards. Also, in order to better understand the action in question, we advance a precept of Liszt which is included among a group of his ideas set forth in Section VI of this chapter. He says: "It is wrong to *fall on* or to *throw towards* the key one wants to reach."[74]

The word *throw* cannot be misunderstood. In piano playing, to *throw* indicates a gesture going away from the axis of the body. Supination is

---

[74]F. H. Clark, op. cit.

the natural result of this action of abduction.[75] On the contrary, adduction invites the act of pronation through its direction towards the axis of the body, even if this gesture continues and passes the axis.

From the fifth measure on of *la Campanella,* the picture of the action makes itself clear. By phrasing from top to bottom and not from bottom to top, one avoids throwing, and thus the precision of the notes in the treble is obtained. The problem here is one of phrasing between a tone in the high treble and one in the middle register.

In the following example one finds confirmation of the validity of our phrasing from top to bottom in the fact that the notes in the treble are *staccato* sixteenths, while the result of the phrasing occurs on eighth notes, consequently less brief. Inverse phrasing between the two notes would irresistibly lead to a "throwing" action by reason of the brevity of the top tone's *staccato.* In this case, the uncertainty of consistently attaining with precision that top note will convince any pianist that such practice is a waste of time. Below are the measures in question, along with the phrasing to be applied, a phrasing which will become imperceptible in the final execution.

By directing the phrasing in this manner, the execution becomes easy. One perceives that little by little the fifth finger, instead of being thrown towards the *staccato* eighth notes, begins to place itself, by pronation, on the high keys. It is then that this pronation, still primitive, is as a result simply prolonged in the direction of the thumb. During this placing one will think about the fifth finger, always after the inward rolling of the shoulder and arm. In the following example, one finds little ornamental notes called *appoggiatura.* These little notes are of great importance for the execution of the whole. The *appoggiatura* is not a note that one flees.

phrase en pronation

[75] See nomenclature, (page 57.)

Moreover, by the rolling maneuver (which consists of mentally making the least of the key to be depressed, in order to eliminate any complex of resistance in the action), these little notes are played without difficulty, inclining lightly with the finger which has just played, to draw afterwards the *appoggiatura* in the direction of the body. In our example, the key which offers a support on which one can lean is very far away from the preceding note. This distance does not hinder one from a slanting crouch on the D sharp, above all when one thinks of the rotating of the shoulder and the arm. In doing this, without the least contraction and with an easy gesture, one realizes that the movement of continuous rotation imposes itself inevitably.

The turning motion which prepares the *appoggiatura* from a great distance, as well as its actual execution in a minuscule movement, is nothing more than an application of the experiment of oblique fall, adjusted to the functioning of the organism which includes the back, shoulder, arm, forearm and hand. Next is introduced a new aspect of the chromatic scale for five fingers, fingering propagated by Busoni. Here is this scale in the First Paganini-Liszt Etude:

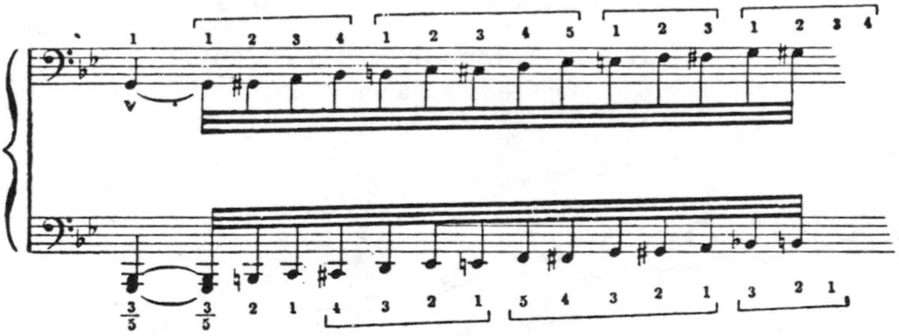

If, while practicing, one introduces before each note of this scale a note for the fifth finger which will serve as point of departure for the pronation, reinforced by the turning inwards [*en dedans*] of the arm, the aspect of the scale becomes the following:

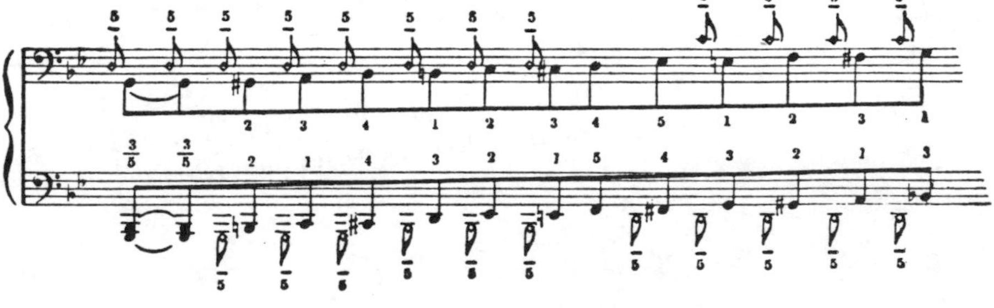

Gamme chromatique montante

1• Étude Paganini - Liszt

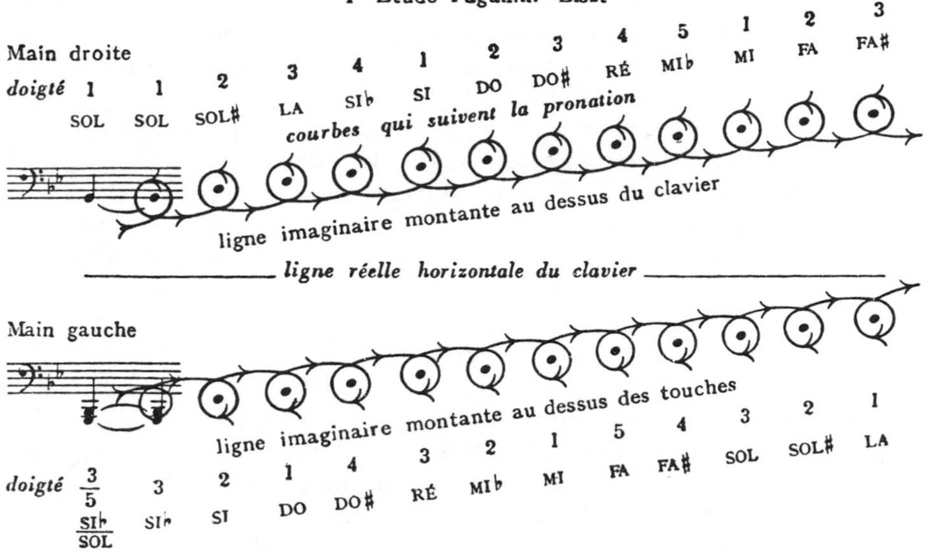

Gamme chromatique descendante

1• Étude Paganini - Liszt

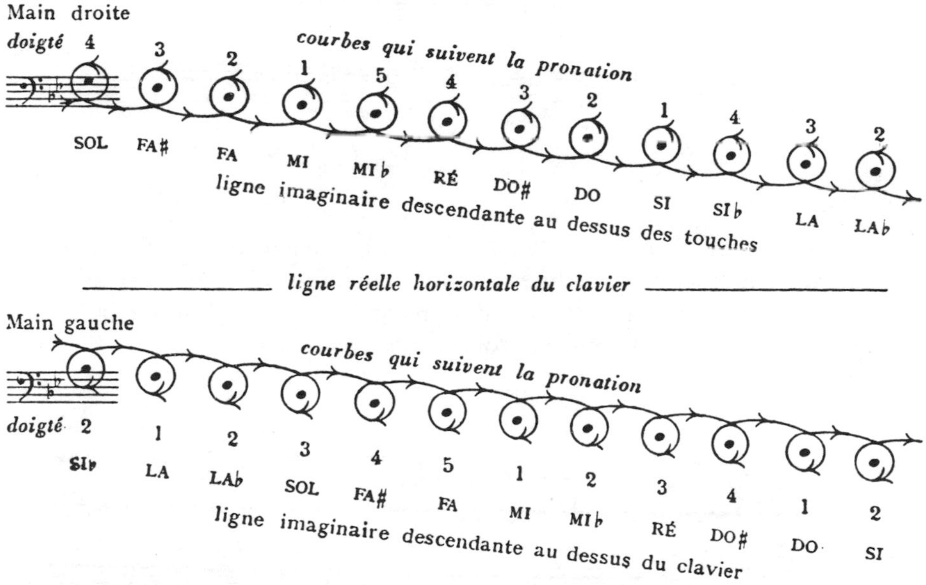

[Translation of directions]

a) Ascending Chromatic Scale, Paganini-Liszt First Etude.
b) Right hand.
c) Fingering:

1	1	2	3	4	1	2	3	4	5	1	2	3
G	G	G♯	A	B♭	B	C	C♯	D	E♭	E	F	F♯

d) Curves which follow the pronation.
e) Imaginary line ascending above the keyboard.
f) Actual horizontal line of the keyboard.
g) Left hand.
h) Imaginary line ascending above the keys.
i) Fingering:

3/5	3	2	1	4	3	2	1	5	4	3	2	1
B♭/G	B♭	B	C	C♯	D	E♭	E	F	F♯	G	G♯	A

[Same scheme for chromatic scale descending]

Executing the scale in this fashion, two converging slopes impose themselves on our imagination. At the place where the thumbs touch the horizontal keyboard, there is outlined for each hand a surface mounting towards the treble. One has the impression, in playing thus, that each finger lowers itself perpendicularly onto this imaginary slope. In reality, the trajectory performed by the finger intersects the imaginary slope by its gyratory movement and the finger attacks obliquely the key that it depresses, to rebound obliquely. Thus, the rotating movement of the playing establishes itself, as is shown in the scheme of the preceding chart.

One finds Busoni's fingering in this chart indicated above the notes.

The circular movement is traced around imaginary sloping lines. As one observes, this movement is directed towards the thumb, ascending and descending.

To more easily accustom the reader to this way of playing through pronation, we cite two examples which will be a revelation for him. While playing these measures, one will have the feeling of never having played them in any other way.

The first of these two examples, the First Ballade of Chopin, op. 23, at its conclusion:

The second, utilizing the common fingering, is Chopin's Etude, op. 25, no. 5.

From this point on, one realizes that supination is more and more eliminated from the actual playing of the piano. It is however important to make provision for supination as well as many other movements which can become superfluous or even detrimental, in order that nothing becomes rusty within the pianist's system.

If the latter two examples likely quell some objections to the supremacy of pronation, there are others which fortify this birth of conviction. And here are some of them. If one recalls the chromatic scale with the action of the fifth finger intercalated,[76] the measure which is reproduced below, taken from *la Campanella,* proves a striking consequence:

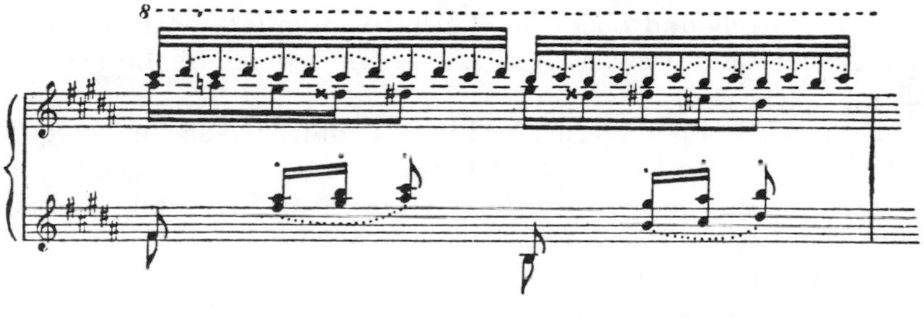

This step leads directly to the execution of the trill and to that of the tremolo.

A trill on two neighboring tones is performed by the isolated action of these two notes. When one must execute a trill on A - G, using the third and second fingers, one commences with a simple vertical bounding on the A, without thinking about the note which follows, all the while not losing tactile contact with the ivory. In holding the third finger ready

[76]See nomenclature, (page 58.)

to descend and rebound, one does the same thing with the index finger on the G. One avoids all tendency to constrict the two notes and one takes care that the movement of each of the fingers is produced, not by the fingers alone, but with the aid of the entire length of the extended arm. When one furiously attacks the keys only, contracting and narrowing the action, one just kills the movement in the egg.

"Why lean over the stupid keys?" says Liszt. "Draw back the body in order to draw back the action!"

Accelerating a little, still without *thinking trill,* one will lightly accentuate the A, and one will concentrate on the trill, slowly prepared, in Beethoven's *Pastoral* Symphony; that trill which introduces the cuckoo's song. There also, at the beginning, the phrasing of the two notes is from the high towards the low.

Relinquishing the distraction of these seductive measures, we concentrate on our trill at the piano. The maneuver of this "pre-trill" is clearly a pronation and to examine its breadth, exactly as we did in the chromatic scale, we intercalate the lower note from which this action stems.

Let us try also, either the fourth or fifth finger. By using these outer fingers, pronation of the hand is emphasized by enlarging the action, drawing it up the arm to the shoulder. After removing the intercalated finger of support, one continues the exercise, first in eighth notes, then in triplets, after that sixteenth notes, and so on. After these pre-exercises, the trill will become an easy thing and the two notes will strike, even with the greatest rapidity, on condition that one does not shift the action towards the tips of the fingers.

Execution of the tremolo is identical.

Measure 51 of *la Campanella* offers a combined example of pronation at a great distance [far enough from keyboard in order that use of the fully extended arm is involved], plus covering of the thumb by the hand, execution of which becomes as follows:

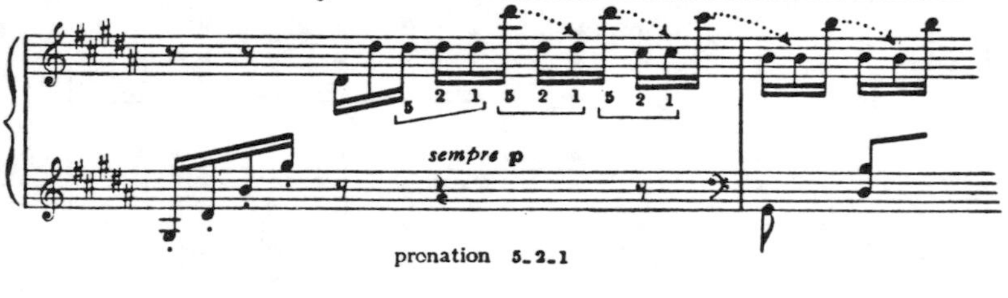

A typical example of the rolling towards the thumb is given by Busoni in the execution by the two hands of the following passage.

Notice especially the two notes played by the left hand, which thus leaves to the right hand the possibility of a free roll inwards:

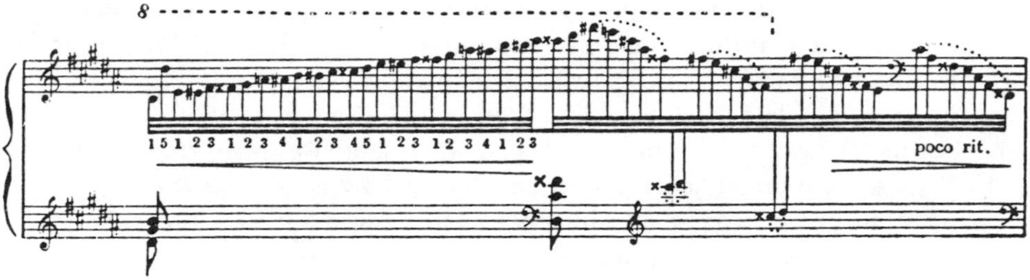

Eleven measures from the end, the left hand plays a repeated ascent of octaves, and this was the opportunity for Busoni and Eugene d'Albert to play this impetuous passage by eliminating the lower G sharp from the third octave. The exhilaration achieved by taking off from the G sharp to the octave on D sharp was a triumph. The ascents of the left hand therefore assumed the following aspect:

One finds this kind of pronation again in many a transcription of Bach by Busoni, among others in the *Chaconne.*

La Chaconne, de Bach *(mesures 41 à 46)* par Busoni

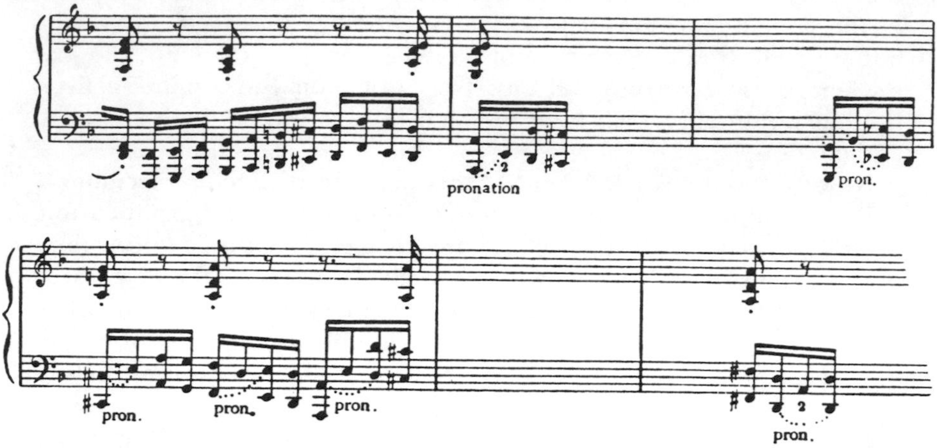

The more one studies *la Campanella* the more one clearly sees the outline of the theory. We repeat the definition given of it previously, in Chapter Two, as well as the point of departure.

"The basis of the act of piano playing is the playing table beneath the keys. Added to this fundament, or point of departure, are two natural laws easily adaptable to the physical commands of the pianist. *These principles being understood, one can build on this initial ground a system of regulated movements by applying the process to a method which sets the elements in a logical progressive order so as to arrive at the only goal possible."*

We have now seen how Liszt reached it. But the ultimate results of the reconstruction of his playing stretch out, projecting infinitely into the purely musical domain toward other "lagoons," toward other seas which have no shores. One should wish to recall the impressions of the two friends listening to the bells of St. Marks, impressions that were described in the Prologue.

We come to the end of *la Campanella,* and further on the concluding measures are reproduced in order to study them particularly. In summing up the contents of this section of "The Birth of a Method," we permit ourselves to say that we have witnessed the construction of the framework. But for a method to be a live one, it must have a soul to animate it; this is its whole reason for being.

The last two pages of the Third Paganini-Liszt Etude represent for many musicians a simple repetition of rapid notes, a virtuosity of doubtful taste.

This opinion stems from the use of an energetic wrist technique, in other words, an action directed towards the keys only. The beginning of Beethoven's *Waldstein* Sonata, op. 53, played in this manner, would present the same "triviality." However, if one thinks of this phenomenon:

that either a diffuse light or an irradiating sound can evoke a sensation of the same diaphanous nature, the execution of these pages begins to outline itself. It will be achieved by a rapidly repeated rebound, allowing the keys to rise again only half-way. The irradiation thus obtained reflects the musical intent which is, at one and the same time, both sparkling and dazzling.

Now to study the melodic line of the theme relative to its execution.

Bear in mind that Liszt executed his scales by motifs grouped into several phrases. By thus designing a sequence of rhythmic undulations in this extensive octave passage, one suddenly discovers the true visage of the Lisztian conceptions. Using the irradiating execution of these octaves, combined with the oblique direction of pronation according to the design of the melodic line, any problem of rhythm resolves itself in all its profound significance.

As in the preceding examples, the indications of phrasing toward the pronation are supplied.

NON-STOCK
OCK

	ACCOUNT NO.	B & T ORDER NO.	ORDER CLASS	ADJ. CODE
19/82 E	U352732	215811	0	M
(1)	(2) (8)	(9) (14)	(15)	(16)

ITEM NO. 001065 (22) N (23)

TITLE ID NO. (24) (31)

EDITION XXXX (32)

TITLE SEARCH XXXXXXXXXXXXXXXXXXXXXXXXX (44)

BATCH (79) (80)

SC –

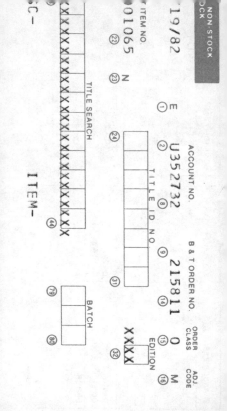

ITEM–

TRANSCRIBER	KEYPUNCH	DATA CONTROL B299	DATA CONTROL B320
		ERROR	ERROR O.K.

DATA CONTROL B240	DATA CONTROL B15	ON FILE LISTED ON B20
ERROR	ERROR	

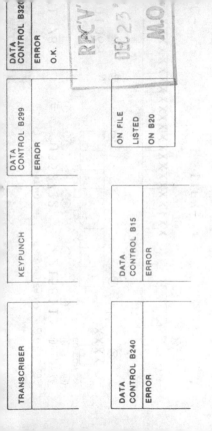

Technique based on the simple natural laws penetrates the domain of music, a domain spiritual. The genius in Liszt thus realized the oneness of execution and thought, *conceived through the musical work.*

From which of these two planes, then, springs the master idea?

It is sheer evidence that this man, whose spirituality directed the whole of his being, found in the execution a reflection of the musical thought; *it was the music which revealed to him the secrets of the technical action.*

At the beginning of this chapter the inverse order was deliberately followed to the moment when evidence of the primacy of the music itself would become apparent. Let the reader please recall the preceding chapters in which this transfer was already presenting itself.

Let us summarize this assemblage of acquired knowledge and examine, in their light, the measures reproduced above.

Through the curving line of the melody, the flight of sound rises and spreads out in a whirlpool of images, some far off, some close.

The prodigious recoil of tempo, in its "immediate presence," resolves itself in a nucleus of bell sounds. Finally, the sound disperses into silences which seem interrogative. One last chord, *pianissimo* and *morendo,* ends the poem.

When one listens to Paganini's music, music haunted by the vertigo of space which engenders the desire for solitude, one understands the affinity which was established between the two men when Liszt heard Paganini's music played by the magician himself.

Liszt was strongly attracted by this man. With Liszt, too, the attraction of space and the desire to detach himself from the world were strong. He, too, was conscious that solitude is no longer burdensome, anguishing, dolorous, as soon as one accepts it. It is from solitude that joy springs, the generous and peaceful conviction of power. Let us heed this tranquil voice, wholly alive and always fresh, when he speaks of his way of playing triumphantly conquered.

VI.

Open wide the windows, so the vibrating air of a beautiful morning in Weimar may put us into the ambiance of the prodigious lessons Liszt gave his pupils.

One of his most astounding proposals was reported to us by his pupil [sic] Clark:[77]

[77]F. H. Clark, op. cit.

"The idea and the effort must be firmly joined to the desire that is within us, in order to render our being conscious of its universality, and to develop our individual liberty far from everything artificial. Only the truly harmonious man who has known how to identify his thoughts, his feelings and his acts with the great forces of nature, is capable of conceiving and of realizing an art in intimate relation with the supreme harmony of the Cosmos, reflected in the supreme harmony of the spirit . . . One does not play the piano with the fingers nor with the hands, but also with the arm, the back, the heart, the whole being.

"The *élan* of the touch is manifested in the arms become hands and fingers. The hands are like the radiating outwards in gestures from the human centre which is, from the organic and corporeal point of view, the heart.

"My art is always directed towards harmony. Now, harmony is the expression of a coordination. The source of my art rises from the ground of the heart, the nervous plexus and the central forces which reside around the vertebral column . . ."

It is not at all necessary to emphasize that we find ourselves in the presence of a radical reversal of traditional practices. But let us return to what has been our point of departure, the purely technical approach by which we analyze and clarify Liszt's thought.

We have demonstrated in the course of this chapter that with him the action begins at the table of playing.

It is not in grazing the ivory that "the *élan* of the touch manifests itself in the arms become hands and fingers," but only in the contact with the solid support which the bottom of the key offers. This support alone permits "the movement which is spread to the entire length of the playing organism."[78]

The example of the revealing fingering which we have given is a witness to this. It provides proof of the existence of the reject (bounce) in Liszt's playing. On condition that the arm be extended, the whole brachial apparatus[79] "becomes hand and fingers."

Digital sensitivity is concentrated first in the middle of the first phalange of the fingers. Liszt speaks of it in the following manner:

"My art is based, as to execution, on the commands of the human body. It emanates from digital sensitivity and considers this last as determinant for the corporeal contact in the execution."[80]

Next, this sensitivity communicates itself simultaneously to two poles, or centres of action. The first resides in the palm of the hand and extends

---

[78]F. H. Clark, op. cit.

[79]See nomenclature (page 57.)

[80]F. H. Clark, op. cit.

up into the underpart of the forearm; the second is found in the shoulder and the arm.

This entire sort of playing within the ensemble of these various components set forth in the text is unthinkable without the primary utilization of the table of playing. We wrote in *l'Élément fondamental de la Technique du jeu chez Liszt et Chopin:*[81]

"For Chopin and Liszt, the table of playing, the bottom of the keys, therefore a fixed base, *was the point of departure of all action; the action takes life from a solid foundation.* In the method of all the other schools, the table of playing is *on the contrary the result, the termination of the action. The action dies in the keys.*"

Not only the example of the revealing fingering given here, chosen from among so many others, is the proof of it; but also Chopin speaks of pillars and points of support when he refers to the functioning of the fingers. Equally with Liszt and with Chopin, every attack is subordinated to the bounce and to the rebound.

Consider an analogous conception in the famous rough draft in Chopin's handwriting, discovered by Alfred Cortot in 1936, lent by him [1937] to the "George Sand and Her Friends Exposition," in the rooms of the Polish Library, and found in the catalogue as No. 179:

> "It is necessary to play the black keys *by pressing them.* (Emphasis ours [Roës]). The wrist, forearm, arm, all will follow the hand according to the sequence, rounding in a curve which gives a degree of most ease, depending on the shape of the hand, *something which the hand could not do if the fingers were extended*"[82] (Emphasis ours [Roës]).

We have amply seen all along this chapter the opposition between pressing and extending.

These words of Chopin agree perfectly with what we wrote in *l'Élément Fondamental* published a year earlier.[83] One finds on page 27 the following conclusion:

"It is clear that in this ensemble of movements, it is neither the shoulder, nor the back which conducts, but the hand; and the organs function afterwards in their ensemble."

---

[81]Henry Lemoine & Co., ed., Paris, 1937

[82]To emphasize the meaning of this quotation we remind the reader that the ideal position according to Chopin is the following: the five fingers on E - F# - G# - A# - B.

[83]*Ed. note:* Marie Stuart de Backer states as follows:

"Cortot's discovery may have been in 1936 (so I heard in England at Reed's) but he did not make it public until the Exhibition at the Polish Library in November 1937. Roës' book, *l'Élément Fondamental,* is dated March 1937. He only saw the manuscript at the Exhibition. I well remember these facts, and I have the programme of the Polish Exhibition where I gave a short lecture on the subject to my pupils."

Liszt, in speaking of this ensemble of organs, pursues his research in order to reach the innermost secret of his playing when he speaks of "movements in spiral, gyratory, twisting":[84]

"The radiating outwards of the force is (consequently) only possible by means of spiral movements, twisting out from the shoulder, elbow and from the hand. Then one obtains a unity of movement which is preserved in every detail.

"For this reason, it is reprehensible to begin the study by aspiring to develop every separate element involved in the whole operation, for example: the exercises of the fingers, the hand and the arm. Any practice which makes a standard habit of hitting the keys by throwing, or falling down on them, is for that purpose only already wrong, since it interrupts the compelling flow and the brilliance of the whole; also for the reason that it separates the unity of the labor, it becomes simply an imitation, prolonged, of the mechanical action of the hammers . . ."

We have seen in the course of this chapter, particularly by testing the bounce in curves, the birth of the *Wirbel-Impuls.*

A little further on, in the same text mentioned above, Liszt explains to us the importance of this *Wirbel-Impuls* (turning):

"The shaping of this *Wirbel-Impuls* continues the production of the movement once it is launched. Thus do I obtain the absolute unity of the movements of the whole brachial apparatus and the rhythmic form of the music: episode, melody, motif, the triple composite of the rhythmic forms with relation to the trinity of the *Wirbel-Impuls,* shoulder, elbow and hand. It is thus that I obtain a harmonious and fluid technique . . ."

One will notice that the succession—episode, melody and motif—corresponds to the succession—shoulder, elbow and hand. What clairvoyance in this imagination, what order in the sequence of his ideas! Starting with the movement of the back, wide in its sweep, passing to the movement of the elbow to the subtle movement of the fingers, Liszt transposes these phases to the episode, which is long, to the melody, less long, and to the motif, which is composed of only a few notes.

One thinks involuntarily of the resemblance of the "infinitely large" and the "infinitely small" and this makes more meaningful his words:

"Only the truly harmonious man, who has the wisdom to identify his thoughts, his feelings and his acts with the great forces of nature, is capable of conceiving and fulfilling an art in intimate rapport with the supreme harmony of the Cosmos reflected in the supreme harmony of the spirit."

Let us now sum up the characteristics of the act of playing according to the method set forth above.

---

[84]F. H. Clark, op. cit.

All movements are conceived as of great span. The imagined space around the gestures extends far beyond the studio in all dimensions. However invisible is the amplitude of the gestures, the feeling of space must be inherent within the reduced movements. The flexibility of the physical ensemble permits execution of these actions of large sweep within a minimum of space as they borrow from the lofty expanse around them. First the free fall, even if in reality executed rather close to key-level, seems in thought to come from an infinitely greater height. Next, the temporary arrest on the key without pushing it down, as a bird lands, provoked by the portative forces of the back and shoulder, is felt as an action which engages the whole body. By this momentary arrest the spiral movement, the *Wirbel-Impuls,* is instantly provoked in the organism of the back. This movement of rotation which is born will be definitively accentuated when the descending mass makes contact with the bottom of the key. There, when the key is completely depressed, the *Wirbel-Impuls* reinforces itself during the bounce and the gyratory movement flashes back towards its source which resides in the back and the shoulder. If one designates this last point as pole B, and the bottom of the key pole A, A being the point where the digital sensitivity manifests itself in its full intensity, one holds in a vision that which in reality the picture of Liszt suggests.

The ensemble of this action, in thought always of great expansiveness, will be reduced then to the real movements hidden in the suppleness of the hand, and one will arrive at creating the playing *with the high arched vault,*[85] while keeping the wrist and the elbow in a low position. This playing with perfect suppleness, but not necessarily spectacular, is a complement and not an element properly speaking, of the construction of the method. We will devote a section of the next chapter to treating its consequences and its application.

To analyze, one sees therefore that the general action has three phases. (1), that in the space above the keybed; (2), that of the descent to the keys; (3), that of the counterreaction at the bottom, that is to say, the bounce taking off from the depressed keys which form the table of playing, that line of definitive arrest of the descent. The sum of these three phases, translated by the expression *"poser le jeu,"* [to place, or placing the playing], gives the perfect preparation of a sonority which is both mellow and powerful, without harshness, by a movement without crispation, but easy and fluid according to Liszt's expression.

We have seen the birth of an action, a sequence of movements, which finds its full development in a circular movement of which the ensemble of the hand and of the arm is *at first the instigator, then the object,* all of

---

[85]See nomenclature, (page 59.)

this being the consequence of the digital sensitivity stimulated under the influence of gravity; the ensemble being directed by the spirit of an orchestra conductor, who in his turn acts according to his inspirations.

* * *

A witness of Liszt's playing is given us by Mme. Auguste Boissier. She relates that:

"His fingers, never curved but not totally flat, seemed to be glued to the keys and did not in any manner hit at them."[86]

This aspect must appear still more astounding to pianists who raise their fingers, if they consider that Liszt had scarcely any acquaintance with pianos with double escapement, that is to say possessing the mechanism which permits the half-descended hammer and the half-rising key to remain in position for playing. This possibility of immediate replaying was therefore already present in his playing technique.

In the following chapter will be explained, with reference to application of the method, how the fingers, finding themselves at the extremity of the living reed, the arm, can be led through progressively releasing the light tension of this flexible reed, to the most rapid sort of repetition, using only a part of the distance travelled by the keys. And this is achieved through the rebound on the table of playing.

Says Liszt, "I find this playing in Chopin. He plays with the arms almost completely extended, his body leaning lightly back, his arms making undulatory movements which are almost imperceptible."

Liszt conceived a way of playing which proved evidence for his method. Chopin practised it without realizing it, while always seeking to define it. Liszt discovered it by his clairvoyance, Chopin was constantly plunged into his experiments.

One is often inclined to think that Liszt was the searcher and Chopin the intuitive one; history, and their works demonstrate the contrary.

There is in the life of these two friends a reciprocal appreciation which has contributed infinitely more to the art of the piano than all the efforts of the most eminent among us.

Their affinity of ideas, their devotion, their admirations and their total unselfishness accomplished marvels. It is moving to see our two friends reunited in the same picture. It is Chopin who is at the piano and Liszt leans over his playing.

For hours on end, Liszt listens and observes. One is tempted to ask him: "What do you hear? what do you see?" and one can perceive a voice which, instead of answering, speaks only to himself:

---

[86]Mme. Auguste Boissier, Franz Liszt as Teacher, Paul Zsolnay Verlag, Berlin.

"This *rubato* . . . what beauty and what result, as logical as it is prodigious, of this undulatory movement! One hand plays a running passage which becomes always melody . . . More rapid in the beginning, it glides as it slows down towards the end . . . This hand plays always outside the beat . . . it is the other which plays implacably *a tempo.* The hands begin together, they also finish together . . . never in the middle of the phrase . . . The young Anton Rubinstein justly remarked that the pedal was deliberately applied in defiance of all the rules . . . There is a multitude of different sonorities which alter the impression of speed . . . one could believe he saw a movement of unformed spots of light on a piece of turf when the rays of the sun are playing through the foliage of a tree cradled by the wind . . . This *rubato* . . . would it be a play of lights and shadows suggested by the hearing? Sometimes the music disengages itself, escapes from its own means of expression . . . Ah! who could paint a picture of the ineffable enchantment of this poetry? . . ."

In a very beautiful sentence, Ignace Paderewski allows us to perceive the answer:

"We can ask it of Him who unveils the bosom of the heart . . . He has not yet told us all . . . and may He never tell us all!"

CHAPTER FIVE

Application of the Method and of the Ideas of the School of Weimar Through a Series of Lessons

These sessions will be preceded by three illustrations of the teaching of Busoni, Eugene d'Albert and Godowsky, masters of the great epoch after the Weimar years.

It is solely love of the art and its teaching that guides this author. One should never hesitate to stand firm against the backward opinions stemming from ingrained habits, or those due to infiltration of the undesirable aspects of contemporary times.

We do not flatter ourselves that we can change opinions which have been fixed for some generations. Those who are stubborn will do well to close this book before reading this chapter. If, on the other hand, some wish to listen to counsels which have been transmitted to us by the disciples of Liszt, let them have the courage to sweep away for a few moments their knowledge and even forget their position among the ranks of artists, while searching loyally to gain that knowledge which is acquired, as Liszt said, "by right of conquest."

For those readers who are of goodwill and also animated by curiosity, we will be present together at these lessons in which the author will take sometimes an active role, sometimes the role of an observer.

The Teaching of Ferruccio Busoni

In order to give a clear idea of his manner of teaching, we must put into relief some significant aspects of Busoni's person. His admiration for the master of Weimar was unlimited. Parallel to his research into the work left by Liszt, the homage to his predecessor is manifested clearly in the art of playing his instrument. His intelligence permitted him to embrace the whole literature for the piano and his executions were, through the application of *"non-legato,"* of a blinding clarity. He knew a glory as no other man. Busoni was not, properly speaking, a pupil of Liszt but, attracted to him, he strove from youth to penetrate Liszt's personality and even his beliefs.

However, Busoni was a Renaissance man, and in his incursions into the domain of the mystical, he would refer only to his intelligence. An evidence of these researches is given to us in the last sentence of his

essay: "Sketch for a New Aesthetic of the Art of Music,"[87] where he speaks of the way of life which he has traced:

"Up to the door which separates man from eternity, only the wanderer—that we are—who knows how to untie the bonds which hold him captive in this terrestrial life, only this Pilgrim sees the door open itself to the kingdom where music, which is no longer the art of music, makes itself heard."

Liszt would have expressed this thought such as Diotime in his dialogue with Socrates:[88]

". . . When, from inferior beauties, one has elevated himself to this perfect beauty and begins to perceive it, he has almost reached the goal . . ."

If there are some differences between the convictions of Liszt and Busoni, they have, all the same, a point in common. Everything Liszt discovered in the domain of instrumental execution was followed, continued and extended by Busoni. And so their manner of teaching was the same. They both understood that to awaken the self-educator in the pupil is the sole good precept to follow. Busoni's lessons consisted of his presence, his gift of suggestion, the example of his playing. Such teaching amounted to a *triage* of those students who immediately caught the deep meaning and those who missed it. Besides, often the grain would germinate after several years.

The results of Liszt's teaching were certainly more immediate. The impressive number of illustrious pianists having followed his course is the proof of it. Their master had formulated for himself his intentions in a very clear manner, based on the conviction which guided him constantly. Thus his technical findings, which he shared with Chopin, aroused all the enthusiasm of the un-instructed.

Busoni on the other hand explored the domain of technique up to the end of his life and people were sometimes troubled when he openly admitted it. However, this gave an inestimable advantage to those who were working with him. They were present at a fecund evolution, characteristic of the whole creation. It was exactly this element, proper to this man of the Renaissance, which was a life-giving stimulant for the new generation, and which today will furnish light on the still obscure route which leads to Weimar. It is so wonderful to see renewal operating as life unrolls! Knowledge which has been acquired gets lost, only to be rediscovered with renewed enthusiasm.

Was not one quite a little perplexed when Busoni used to say: "What I seek is a technique constructed on a stable base"? For, as one watched

---

[87] *Esquisse d'une nouvelle esthétique de l'art musical,* Insel-Verlag, Leipzig.

[88] Plato, The Banquet.

him play, one was inclined to ask him, "What do you mean? . . . it is already there, the stable base! . . . Your *non-legato,* is it anything other than a rebound from the base under the keyboard"?

However, Busoni never mentioned the word "rebound," nor the word "fulcrum" [point of support] to designate the table of playing, the fixed base under the keys. This was neither negligence nor the desire to keep a secret. In evoking the personality of Busoni one ponders: what is this unfathomable element which always conceals the obvious? Now, what movements did he make that he did not explain!

An example of his suggestive method:

In order to teach control of the journey of the descending key, while realizing its difficulty for the pupil, he simply said: "I hear the shock of your fingers on the keys, which ought not to be." This observation forced one either not to leave the key, or to arrive on the key after having interrupted the fall; in other words: *to place one's playing.*

He contented himself with observing the results of his remarks, on the watch for the least alteration which might proceed from the activity of other parts of the body.

Nothing escaped this fine observer.

* * *

A typical habit was the manner in which he sat before his instrument while playing. One noticed that he often made rising and descending motions, as if he were riding horseback on his chair. A deceptive motion for those who saw in it a mannerism. It was exactly the opposite of what one thought it to be; it was a constant need to sit down again heavily, it was not at all a gesture for the purpose of rising intermittently. Later on, some individuals learned that to "sit down heavily," "to press the back on the chair," is the first condition for obtaining a light hand, the hand which is then carried by the outstretched arm regulating its own weight and taking its strength from the pressing down of the back muscles.

The light hand; the inactive wrist; the extended arm which is suspended and weighing down; the heavy, compact back; this formula forms the basis of a technique which allows both for light playing and for greatest power.

This attitude of body of Busoni corresponds perfectly with that which Clara Wieck noticed, to her great astonishment, in Liszt:

". . . From time to time he slumps down in front of his piano."

Busoni never spoke about this body position, nor of its consequences, but one day he said, with a wink, to one of his students: "Is it not true that it is wrong to always practice in a *forte* manner?"

In one of the lessons which are to follow in this series, we will return more explicitly to a fact of unique significance. All of Busoni's disciples have in their playing one characteristic in common with him: the kind of sonority which is augmented as the action releases the keys, instead of diminished. With these musicians, the sound is not stifled in the instrument, it takes flight into space. According to Busoni's precepts, the weight must not continue to exert pressure on the key; the key must be allowed to rise slightly, through the influence of the lightening of the arms by the back, in such a manner that the hammer remains floating, approaching the strings without at the same time touching them again. At this moment one realizes that the sound, through an effect which we leave to acousticians the task of explaining, is amplified very considerably, and resumes new flight. The deployment of sonorities Busoni had at his command was particularly admirable. His manner of playing *carried* the sound without ever being superfluous. Even those who were not connoisseurs were struck by the perfection of the means he used to obtain the exact sonority he wanted. This appeared to them as an incontestable truth. His idea was: to carry the sound, to accompany it a moment toward the heights.

* * *

The tradition of Weimar was for Busoni the framework for every day. The author remembers, as if it were yesterday, his first visit to Busoni who was then at the apogee of his fame. The welcome was worthy of the most beautiful traditions at Liszt's auditions in Weimar. Busoni apologized for the condition of his two pianos which were, however, in excellent condition. "Try them, and you will see that it will be a little difficult to do justice to yourself on them." The kindness which emanated from this pianist with such great psychological gifts immediately had its calming effect. It was an invitation to play calmly. A sort of pacifying for the purpose of avoiding a nervous execution.

Moreover, in the center of a world of admirers, he stood alone with his immense knowledge. Some of his intimates read in his eyes the sadness of one who knew that even the most eminent power does not render a man happy as long as it is destined he remain prisoner in that which he himself called the bonds of terrestrial life. His glance showed us that everything appeared to him under a nostalgic light, but his magnificent bearing taught us to confront life as a free man. His pianistic genius taught us that he who listens to us in the right spirit is at that moment our only companion on the road which, in spite of the diversity of circumstances, leads us toward the same goal.

An Extraordinary Lesson

On a day when Leopold Godowsky relaxed after his concert the previous evening, it was announced to him that a man about forty years of age who did not wish to give his name desired to speak to him. A little intrigued by the anonymity of his visitor, Godowsky told his servant to have him enter. The mysterious personage was brought into the studio and Godowsky saw approaching him, Sergey Rachmaninoff.

—What an agreeable surprise, my dear colleague! What brings you to my house?

—It is an honor to meet you again and I am going to tell you immediately the reason for my visit. I so admired your playing during your concert last evening that I am asking you please to give me what I would like to call a lesson.

Godowsky, flattered but completely mystified, asked his visitor to be seated and to explain to him his strange request.

—You are a wonderful pianist and known all over the world!

Turning a deaf ear to the compliment, Rachmaninoff answered:

—I observed in your left hand something I have never seen in any other pianist and that I myself do not possess. Would you be generous enough to reveal your secret to me?

Godowsky was surprised, but the calm of his compatriot was so imposing, and the humble request so sincere, that after some hesitation, he began, according to his habit, to speak volubly:

—I am left-handed and perhaps it was that which made you notice that I carry the left hand with great facility towards the middle of the keyboard (while applying naturally a light *crescendo* as I ascend towards the treble in order to remedy the weakness of the instrument), while in general it is with the right hand that one plays in the powerful register in the middle, and with the left in the bass, which is already very sonorous.

—If I understand you correctly, you maintain, as in the orchestra, a sonorous mass coming from the bass of the piano and covering three quarters of the keyboard, and you play in the treble by attacking the key from a small height, which produces the timbre of high-pitched instruments calling for a light attack.

A broad smile from Godowsky accompanied several words of admiration for a colleague who, thanks to his fine ear, had so well grasped the power of pronation,[89] and he said to him:

---

[89]See nomenclature, (page 59.)

—I accept with pleasure your compliment, but I must say to you that your right hand surpasses mine in clarity. You have, in your right hand, that light attack from a short distance, without throwing towards the treble.

The pianists exchanged glances with the air of accomplices.

—Of course, we are speaking about the same thing; it was necessary simply to realize that with your prolonged pronation of the left hand, you maintain a perfect equilibrium between the bass and the treble which is the least sonorous part of the keyboard.

—For a left-handed person like myself, this equalization is executed naturally. For you who need to strive for perfect equilibrium between the two hands it is the ear alone which must establish it. The left hand soon follows easily because, even with a non-left-hander, it is the strongest, although in general less dexterous. It is certainly significant that my left hand plays absolutely glued to the keys and that from time to time my right hand executes, as you say, the attack at a light distance. And is it not amusing to juggle with the keys which can thus be transformed into instruments?

When, twenty-five years later, Rachmaninoff told us of his visit to Godowsky, he glided modestly over the remaining course of his conversation with the greatest technician of the epoch.

The lesson that can be drawn from this encounter is the fact that Rachmaninoff, at the age of forty-five years, did not hesitate to study the playing of his *confrères* and consult them, a habit he kept all his life. But this man had the rare virtue of never criticizing another artist; he always found a word of praise, sincerely convinced that everyone works seriously and with his whole heart. Such a person was Rachmaninoff who, through his professor, Siloti—himself a student of Liszt—continued the tradition of Weimar.

An Impromptu Lesson, Resulting Unexpectedly from an Indiscretion

This happened in Vienna where a young pianist was to give a concert two days hence. He went to the firm of Bösendorfer, celebrated piano manufacturer, to practice. In the corridor, before entering his studio, he heard someone playing behind the opposite closed door. This playing possessed extraordinary power and its progress was most curious.

Attracted, he paused and listened. Each passage, after a rapid execution, was repeated so slowly and in such a let-down manner that one had the impression that the pianist no longer knew the passage in question;

after having livened up a little bit, the initial speed was never resumed. Then he worked in the same manner some other passages.

Suddenly the playing stopped and the door opened abruptly; the indiscreet one saw a little man with fluttering eyelids appear, who said to him, "Please do me the pleasure of not listening behind the door," then seeing the consternation of the guilty one who had just recognized the amazing pianist Eugene d'Albert, added, "Come on in then, and tell me who you are." The young pianist apologized, gave his name[90] and Eugene d'Albert thoughtfully inclined his head.

—I saw your name on the advertisement this week; it is you who play the day after tomorrow in the concert hall, at the same time as I play?

—Yes Master, that is right.

—Then you can do me a service; if you will sit down I will tell you how.

The unexpected guest complied, happy as he was overcome by the good luck of finding himself, all of a sudden, by the side of that pianist for whom Busoni himself had the highest esteem, a pianist who had been the only one to make such an impression on Busoni. Such an encounter was not one to put the eavesdropper at ease, but d'Albert's good nature, which in no wise diminished his authority, revealed itself. In a confidential tone he resumed:

—Would you like to observe how I free myself from nervousness before a concert? In your presence, I am going to relax my playing completely, which is exactly the contrary of what pianists ordinarily do before playing in public. Here is the *Méphisto* Waltz. I am listening to its division into groups of four measures as Liszt indicates, and I am allowing my playing to follow slowly, always behind what I am hearing. You see that apparently nothing remains of my "command of playing." I allow my hands to go carelessly where they will and it is this reducing of all effort to the minimum which brings on the drifting, the uncertainty. I am playing pretty badly, am I not?

And indeed, this playing of a giant had changed itself into something mushy, as if it were the attempts of a child.

—But then, while you abstain from all effort, are you not meanwhile taking all sorts of risks?

—That is correct, and the debacle is all the more complete because you are present. Nothing is more effective than putting one's nerves to the test of producing the minimum of effort before a concert; nothing

---

[90]*Ed. note:* "The young pianist" was Paul Roës.

is more detrimental than indulging in illusions by forcing effort before a concert.

The young pianist, most humble, thus listened and comprehended the significance of what he had been told, and d'Albert continued for about twenty minutes. Then d'Albert rose, walked around the studio, and said:

—I do this in order to view myself from a distance . . . And believe me, if during a concert one is able to view himself from a distance, then one is truly playing in a disengaged manner. Now, since I have egotistically enlisted you as a "lightning rod witness," to make up for it I shall explain to you certain things.

—I cannot tell you what joy you give me!

—I beg of you. First of all, here in Vienna, accept things with this musical ease which is in the air. If Vienna did not yet exist, I believe that music would construct her. What musicality unfolds itself here from the atmosphere and from the soil! What are you going to play the day after tomorrow?

—Among other things I am playing the *Appassionata.*

His little eyes sparkled. He returned to the piano and played the entire *Appassionata.* The young pianist remembered at this moment a phrase written on the subject of d'Albert's interpretations of the Sonatas op. 53, 57 and 101: "His interpretations will remain an example for generations to come." Imagine the admiration of the young pianist when he heard the initial motif, C, A flat, F, continued and intensified in the sudden burst of the fifteenth measure by an almost imperceptible pause before the E natural which begins the first group of 16th notes, and by a light accent on the first E of the following group! This set the stage in a grand manner for the whole first movement of the Sonata.

Scarcely had d'Albert finished playing the last two chords when he signalled to the young man to remain silent a moment, seeming still to listen to what he had just created.

—You must judge, after playing a piece of very great volume, the silence which follows . . . If there remains the least remembrance of sound, the execution has not been perfect.

As d'Albert, without waiting for a word of admiration from the young pianist, began again to play some passages in his "let-down" manner, the latter had a curious thought: in what manner did this man develop his gigantic interpretations? Until now, his conception was one of a Titan, incarnation of the grand forces of nature, who plunged deep into the thickest of forests, having an innate prowess such as wild beasts possess. At this instant the young man realized that, for this man, the structure

of playing was based on the slow and patient accumulation of basic rudiments, yet completely dominated by his inspiration. After a silence, he dared ask:

—How can you relate the power of your *Appassionata* to the preliminary work and what follows it?

The answer was instantaneous:

—To what force can we resort if it does not emanate from our thoughts? And if, underlying the rhythms, the long tracings and the enormous sonorous masses, there does not abide our frail but otherwise powerful affectivity? You know very well from whom I learned this manner of playing, never forget it.

The name of Liszt had not been mentioned . . . but what silent homage! Eugene d'Albert continued:

—You have certainly noticed that, in the second movement, I played the thirty-second notes as a melody and not as an accompaniment; this should show you that almost the entire Sonata is a continuous melody. Everything ascends in this work, save the final passage.

—I understand what you are saying perfectly and I must tell you that today I have received the lesson of my life . . .

—Don't mention it, for I understand; fortunately we all experience these moments. Before parting, I would like to play for you the Impromptu in G flat major by Schubert. You will hear a superb voice which seems to speak.

Eugene d'Albert's touch modified itself substantially. It seemed to draw more upon the resources of relaxed "*démonté*" playing, above all in the accompanying part. He played the eighth notes of the melody relatively slower than the quarter notes, thus giving to that long melodic line a superhuman tranquility. In the final phrase, one heard a delightful reminiscence of the scene at the spring in Beethoven's *Pastoral* Symphony.

—I have not asked you to play anything for me, for that would not be good for you just before your concert, but I am sure that I will see you again soon. Look you, the one who finishes his recital first must come over to the other one; we are playing in the same building, are we not? Agreed?

—I believe that I am in fact the only one who is able to promise that. I shall come therefore to see you in your dressingroom after the concert to thank you again for your great kindness.

And so it turned out. When the young pianist had finished several encores and received several people in his dressingroom, he found the

other concert hall filled to capacity, a public bursting with enthusiasm, and Eugene d'Albert in the process of playing his "nth" encore: the Impromptu in G flat major by Schubert.

This souvenir of Vienna made an everlasting impression on the young pianist; he often recalled that epoch when the great interpreters were not yet unapproachable.

Practical Application of the Author's Precepts

First Lessons Given to a Pianist
Who Has Not Been Taught According to Liszt's Method[91]

I.

Following his request for an audition, a young man presented himself at the appointed hour. Upon entering the studio he explained why he had come.

—It has been my intention to follow the career of concert pianist, but I commence to fear that this ambition is already jeopardized. I have worked for ten years under the direction of different professors and now my playing is no longer progressing.

—Your impression is that you have reached the limit of your capabilities?

—Exactly, and I want to ask you what I should do, because to abandon my career would be for me irreconcilable.

—Show me a little of what you are doing. Do you have any composition at your fingertips, a prelude or an etude of Chopin? Play with ease as though you were at home and above all do not be concerned if it doesn't go as you would like it to. Simply try my piano. Choose a chair.

—Do you have one which is higher?

—Here is one which may suit you.

The young pianist seated himself, erect at first, then he leaned toward the keyboard and played the Prelude, op. 28, no. 16 of Chopin without a single mistake. He used a finger action, raising them very high above the keys; the left hand octaves were executed from the wrist. The exaggerated rapidity led one to believe that the performer followed the fashion for speed.

---

[91]In order to properly understand these counsels, a complete understanding of the preceding chapter is indispensable.

—Thank you sir. Would you now do me the favor of playing this piece again very slowly, that is to say at half the speed, in the same relaxed manner?

The young man repeated the Prelude, but this time with much less assurance.

—Well! You see, you play very easily when you are in what I call a state of giddiness, consequently you do not listen to what you do. It is the fault of many pianists these days and you are one of that number. Do you want to play something else for me?

—Willingly, but I fear it will not be much better.

—It is more important for us both that you show me your faults rather than trying to make a good impression. Don't be discouraged, for you will see just how instructive faults can be.

The Third Ballade of Chopin was played in exactly the same manner as the Prelude; this time the master did not request a slower execution, for he understood.

—Permit me to ask you several questions. You go to concerts often?

—Yes, and preferably to those of pianists.

—And the next day do you work in the spirit of that which has impressed you?

—Certainly, for it is an inspiration for me.

—I am happy to learn that this stimulates you, but aren't you ever discouraged?

The young man responded with a smile:

—This may seem curious to you, but when I hear fine playing I get a powerful sense of possibilities within myself which, once I resume my practicing, I can no longer grasp.

—To be sure, you have talent but have been misled. With you, what is lacking is the relationship between your goal and the means of obtaining it. Would you have the courage to recognize this gap and to forget for a whole month all that you have done up to this moment; in other words, you consider yourself as a raw beginner who submits to building a natural way of playing without thinking of a career, and without concerning yourself with what others around you think? After this length of time, you can do what you wish.

—It seems to me I am hearing the sound of a bell which each professor . . .

—. . . rings in your ear because he believes that his method alone is the right one.

—Pardon me, but this happens so often.

—Naturally it does; a professor would not be worthy of his title if he did not have this confidence in himself, but today you have rung the doorbell of someone who by principle does not belong to the category of the exclusivists. A natural way of playing does not acknowledge a personal system to be imposed on an individual, but one that is acquired simply by following some laws of nature which have value for all.

—Please believe me if I say I cannot clearly understand what you are telling me until I know your method.

—That is logical and all I can answer is that your experiment, if you want to undertake it, is a question of confidence. Do you accept that?

—You ask me for a month; permit me not only to grant you this trust, but to ask if you will please agree to give me your advice.

—I will be happy to, for I am acquainted with reticence among young people, which I will explain to you later. For the moment, let us continue our lesson. Will you show me how you begin your practice in the morning? Sit down at the piano and proceed as if you had just opened your instrument to work.

The student began with several rapid scales.

—Do you do this every morning?

—Yes, and after that I continue with the particular composition that I want to study.

—Have you heard of the *détente?* [relaxation, letting go]

—Yes.

—And also the free fall? Do you know what that means?

—It means to let fall in a total *détente* the weight of the arm onto the keys; is that what you mean?

—We will see. Will you raise your arms, spread them out horizontally, and then let them fall against your thighs.

The young man did this: his arms fell softly onto his thighs while his body leaned forward; no sound was heard.

—Will you repeat this maneuver without leaning the trunk forward? Hold it straight.

This time the body remained straight, but the arms fell just as softly.

—What you are doing is not a free fall, your arms are constricted if you do not hear a good slap.

Following a correct execution, the student said:

—Indeed, I did not know that I was holding back the free action of the fall.

—Perform this experiment with all your pianist friends and you will discover the same phenomenon. Now that you understand what total *détente* of the arm means, I invite you to do the same thing in the direction of the keyboard; but above all, remain passive and do not add force during the descent. What chord do you choose?

—Let us say, C-E-G.

The arms fell without conviction upon the chord and also on two neighboring notes.

—There is no danger of your breaking my strings.

—It isn't that; I do not yet dare to release myself to an absolute *détente*.

—One question: if already in this simple movement, hesitation and insecurity reign, would you understand that in your playing there is never a complete *détente*?

—I understand it perfectly well, but does one apply this free fall while he is playing?

—Please listen to me carefully. Later I will explain how it is used. For the moment, observe solely what the absence of *détente* in your playing illustrates. This absence permits oppostion of two forces, that of weight [letting down], and that of the resisting force [lifting]. When the arms tighten while letting down, so does the whole playing organism contract. Do the following exercise: begin by letting the hand, carried by the outstretched arm, fall onto the cover of your piano, not on the dropboard which covers the keys, but on the top of the grand piano. Be sure that your body remains straight. For a second exercise, pretend that the cover of the piano is fragile and let your hands and your arms fall freely up to within a centimeter of reaching the cover, so that you do not touch it. If the body remains straight you will perceive that the arresting of the outstretched arm is obtained through the strength of the back and not that of the arm, which must remain a dead weight. The essential thing is to have a strong back and to feel distinctly that it is the back which carries the arm. If you do not feel it yet, sit at an angle before the instrument and, just as a moment ago, let fall your hand, carried by the arm, to the side of the body without bending the elbow. The more you turn the arm towards the rear, the more you will feel the effort of

your back. In applying this to the playing as a permanent habit, the movement will depend more and more upon the action of your back.

—What must I do in the way of practice?

—Enlarge your gestures in this manner and if you play, concentrate on the essentials of this entire action, for it will force you to play slowly and conscientiously. I also recommend that you imitate the movement of a windmill with your arms while your hands try to reach an object as far away as possible. This exercise will be useful only by extreme exertion. Next, with all of this in mind, practice a composition; the particular one is unimportant except that it be completely memorized, since reading the notes distracts one's attention from the movement. Accordingly, continue your work guided by what you have just experienced. You will certainly feel some reaction in the muscles; return only when that has disappeared. If there isn't too much reaction, come back and see me in four days. Don't be afraid, you will not have lessons every four days, but at the beginning it is necessary. Stop the mechanical work of scales. You will play them more easily when listening to their musical meaning. Play the series of rhythmical scales which precede the fugue in Liszt's Sonata; listen to that of the hymn in Beethoven's *Pastoral* Symphony. You will understand that the scale is a melodic expression. If you look through music scores you will find an infinite number of such examples. That is all for today. I wish you good courage.

The young man took his leave and went away most intrigued.

II.

Four days later at the appointed hour, the young pianist returned for his second lesson.

—What is the result of your first experiment?

—Very curious. I followed your advice; I practiced the free fall with the whole arm onto the piano cover, without interruption; and afterwards with the arrest. Then I did the same thing on the keys. This taught me that the difference in height between the cover and the keyboard obliges one to sit lower in order to play.

—You have indeed worked conscientiously, and this has allowed you to draw your own conclusions which are both logical and most important.

—I must tell you that "raising the arm by means of the back" gave me a slight muscular soreness, but that disappeared very soon.

—The reaction proves that you had not been using these muscles. Will you please sit at the piano and leave the dropboard closed. I am going to open it for you. Here is the row of keys in front of you. What is your

first impression as you glance over this row of black and white keys; or rather in what direction are you thinking? From left to right, from right to left, or some other way?

—Your phrase "some other way" suggests to me that it is neither from right to left nor inversely that you see the keyboard.

—That is correct. It may seem unimportant to you to consider which is for yourself the direction of the keys, and yet that is a secret of the progress towards perfection in playing. You have played many scales but have you ever thought of anything besides lateral progression?

—Truthfully, that has been mostly in my mind.

—By repeating scales ad infinitum, you quickly forget that during the process you raise your fingers. But notice that there is between two tones an "interval."[92] During the movement which connects the two tones by the curve which their interval outlines, the hand naturally assumes the form of a vault shaped as a high arch. Now I ask you where this arch rests.

—If I depress two keys simultaneously, it rests on the bottom of the keys.

—And if the two fingers do not rest a moment on the bottom, the arch is suspended and ceases to have this support.

—It is then rather like a horseshoe suspended in air.

—What do you do when you walk? You are not suspended, you attract constantly the same amount of gravity, and you are obliged to consider your legs as two pillars of an arch, each of which rests a moment on the ground. But what happens when you walk forward? You raise one of these pillars, but that does nothing to send you forward. Then you push the ground behind you with the foot which remains as pillar, and at this moment you advance. Understanding the movement of walking teaches that the propelling force is the *push* from the ground behind, not the *lift* of the advancing foot that sends one forward. Transpose this to the keyboard by thinking of "walking" with the hands. Now play a scale, and try once the gesture of pushing back a second onto the bottom of the key and tell me what you feel.

—If I perform the bounce brusquely, the elbow has a tendency to raise itself.

[92] Bear in mind that here, the designation of the word "interval" is not the "distance" between two tones, but the liaison which unites them by a curve, a liaison very sensitive to singers, or those who play stringed instruments.

—And if, at the moment when you feel most strongly the key bed, you oppose the weight of the outstretched arm by exertion of the back muscles, what happens at the exact instant of bouncing? Try it.

—The whole arm springs up each time that I rebound in that way.

—And therefore, you do the reverse of raising the fingers by their own strength, or by means of the wrists, or even by bending the elbow; all of these gaining, nevertheless, sufficient height to replay the very same tone.

—I begin to understand the purpose of a strong back . . .

—all the while considering that the back, having received a signal from the natural spring [the flexors] of the underpart of the hand and forearm (a spring stretched to its extreme by the weight of the fully extended arm), instantly relieves a part of the weight which the elasticity of the hand could not lift solely by itself. First of all remember this: when you raise the fingers only, you are using the extensors, muscles which are five times weaker than the flexors, those which execute the rebound. For example, when you shake the hand of another, you squeeze it with the flexors; you can easily crush it. On the other hand, opening the hand is accomplished by the extensors which have little strength.

—Therefore, the same muscles which raise the fingers also open the hand?

—Yes, and in the first place you see how futile it is to use the weakest, instead of the strongest muscles when playing the piano. One sees the cause of cramps along the outside of the arm where the weaker extensor muscles pass. All the pianists' misery of constricted playing lies there; but today we do not dwell on that matter. Yet you would not be here if you had not been aware of what we have just verified: the feeling of having reached the end of one's technical possibilities.

—I must say to you that it upsets me to think that thousands of piano students are thus handicapped or even doomed to failure.

—I will go even further to say that, besides these, dozens of fine pianists would possess a totally different ease of playing if they took the trouble to study this aspect. Certainly, there are some among them who nevertheless arrive at what is referred to as a great technique, in spite of neglecting the natural laws. First, this technique may not be as great as one thinks; after that, who knows what they might have attained if their natural means had been applied? I will not mention out-of-kilter nerves which can be a consequence of misuse of the muscles; this you can easily picture for yourself.

—I begin to catch a glimpse of a new method . . .

—It is nothing new, Liszt and Chopin played in the only valid manner, but one loses sight of it. Chopin would not have become a great pianist if he had not followed the natural laws. The work he bequeathed to us is significant; he had a minimum of time during his short life to acquire his powerful technique. At present, the issue for you is to learn how to regulate and distribute the action, and I want right now to mention the relation of this action to the ear. Here is a point on which I beg you to reflect: a sightless person does not bump into a wall in front of him; he hears it through his ear, and the sensitivity of his skin has already told him his distance from the wall; accordingly he adjusts his movements. What do you think?

—That I visualize a boundless possibility of a new world of sound.

—Your rewarding answer tells me that I have said enough for today. Through the logic that you demonstrate to me in your replies, I see that you will discover many things for yourself, which is vital for a pianist. Thus you should feel much encouraged. I leave you to your study with no further direction. Prepare for me something that you have previously memorized and return to see me next week.

III.

When the student arrived for his third lesson he manifested some hesitation concerning an accurate functioning of the bounce. And truly, when one tries a brief experiment at the piano, it becomes obvious that the spring of the hand does not react with the same force as the back.

—I would like you to experience the simultaneity of these two reactions through another means. A practical application may give you a stronger conception of it.

" Suppose a narrow band of firm but flexible steel is fastened onto a table with its extreme end extending out from the table edge by a dozen centimeters. A springboard has been created. This of course has very little resemblance to a piano key, the latter having infinitesimal power of rejection. If the fingertip gives pressure intermittently on the very tip of this band while balancing on it, one will notice the forceful lift that it gives to the whole of the finger, hand and extended arm, without aid from the back. It is assumed that your imagination replaces the necessity of having the actual installation under your hand. A diving board furnishes this same impetus to a swimmer when he tests, by bouncing, the amount of spring he needs. Test the spring of this steel band, still with fingertip and fully extended arm, but now moving always closer to the edge of the table. The force of rejection lessens as the fingertip approaches the table, and then the back will become associated with the

muscular effort. This simple experiment will not fail to give your brachial apparatus the feeling of the bounce.

—It is amazing. The balance is automatically adjusted.

—Good, we talk no more about bounce and rebound. The habit will soon take hold. It is only an application of our preceding lesson. Now, I would like to know what you have discovered concerning the influence of the ear on the action.

—I can now hear a *crescendo* after the note is attacked. The sound amplifies when the key has started up a millimeter.

—In other words you hear the sound renewed after its emission. That's perfect. And then?

—Because of this fact, I have felt a greater facility for playing the next note in the same way.

—You have therefore felt the influence of the hearing on the progress of the playing. Thus the ear must acquire its own technique and this latter is the true stimulant, or if you prefer, the true motivation of playing. There is yet another peculiarity which I want to emphasize. Each sound comports within itself a syncopation, that is to say, its prolongation on the weak beat. If you divide, at first, the duration of a sound into four beats, the syncopation is found on the third beat. After having trained your ear to hear the syncopated beat, you will succeed with very little effort in hearing the echo of its syncopation on the second beat. In exerting yourself thus you will succeed in re-hearing the echo before the second beat and finally your ear will perceive this sonorous prolongation almost immediately after the descent of the key. That is the rudimentary way of exercising one's ear. Let your ear rest often, train yourself to hear nothing. This relaxation is in concordance with muscular relaxation. Relax during the day, without even listening to . . . silence. The Orientals give us an example in this domain. Activity and non-activity are two elements which must be present in our playing.
" I have made this suggestion to you to make you understand the importance of the technique of listening.

—For you, the ear is the regulator of the action?

—Precisely, and your experience in listening after the production of the sound will soon lead you to perceive the sonority in advance.

—But one actually does this while going from one note to another!

—Exactly, and it is the moment of fixing, for good, this process of hearing and acting. The ear is the nervous center of all action and it must be able to assure the necessary relaxation for all the action.

—You consider that relaxation of the hearing is as important as that of the physical organism?

—Certainly. Its virtuosity is composed of relaxation and . . . attention. If one listens with a strained ear, one finishes by hearing nothing at all and the playing organism is thrown off the track. One violinist had stage-fright while playing and this manifested itself in his bowing. His ear was too much concentrated on the strings of his instrument. He was counselled simply to try to listen nonchalantly as though from a distance, and actually, the trembling of his bowing ceased. Just a little anecdote which will serve you for a comparison; in this case it was a question of a too-fixed attention.

" This happened in Rembrandt's studio. A visitor was examining a canvas as through a microscope. Rembrandt went up to him, took him by the nose, backed him away while still holding his nose, and said: "My dear sir, the odor of paint is not good for you; try looking from farther away."[93]

" Take this little story as an example from the distant past, that you may be sure to listen at a distance.

—When I think that when I came here I was leaning over the keys . . .

—with the elbow bent, doing the opposite of the conductor who extends his arm and thus extends the action of his orchestra. Liszt and Chopin leaned back so they could hear better. Everything in the musical life is dependent on everything else. Inspiration too, raises its head in order to regard the heights.

—I want very much to show you what I have practiced this week.

—Excellent idea, what are you going to play for me?

And without the least constriction the young pianist played Chopin's Etude, op. 10, no. 6, which in the past had been a part of his repertoire. It was a joy to hear the equilibrium between the beauty of this work and the technique of the execution. The melody sang as if under the violinist's bow and the static accompaniment was like the canvas beneath a painting.

—I let myself be guided by the wide intervals of the melody and by the inexorable advance of the accompaniment. This "static" movement, if one examines the score, is in complete communication with the direction of the piano keys which come towards you; and formerly I did not realize that when one leans over the keyboard this movement totally escapes you.

---

[93]Arnold Houbraken, Rembrandt van Rijn, The Hague, 1753.

—You have enveloped this Etude with an atmosphere which will be useful to you in your future executions. Your hands are already lighter. However, let me tell you this. This tranquil atmosphere requires preparation in the few seconds which precede the execution.

" When you put your hands on the keys before beginning, what do you feel within yourself?

—I hesitate still to play the first notes.

—I could see it.

—Could you explain this hesitation to me?

—Do you remember Liszt's expression: "The arm and the hand become fingers?" In the few seconds before beginning, relax the muscles, thanks to which it will seem to you that the weight of your hands ebbs towards the arms and the back, to the stronger muscles. You thus restore to your fingers their freedom of action. Many pianists do not realize that, in the wait which precedes the execution, a heaviness flows towards their hands, and that this current prevents a normal rapport between the free action and . . . the ear.

—How must this be remedied? Must one listen more, mentally, before beginning?

—That is one of the preparations, but there is still another thing. Do me the favor of rubbing the edge of the white keys with the part of the hand where the wrist begins, at the same time keeping your arm always outstretched.

The pupil executed this order by rubbing from left to right and vice versa the line of the edge of the keys with the palm of his hand.

—No, do it squarely with the part next to the wrist, like this, see, and continue for about a minute while keeping the hand completely lax. What do you feel?

—I feel my whole hand . . .

—. . . and you likewise feel a light fulcrum, ephemeral, I dare say. In order to slide easily, the back must carry more the arm and the hand.

—I really felt it.

—Now, play.

—It is curious, now I feel the ends of the fingers less, and more of the implantation of the fingers in the hand.

—Perfect. The part of the hand with which you rubbed the edge of the keys will be from now on the hyphen between the palm of the hand and the dorsal muscles. This action sharpens the sensibility of the ensemble of the organs in action. You perceive also that this increase of power

will lead you to enlarge the movement in the shoulders, so that your playing expands and attains a span as large as the room where you work and this space integrates itself into the action. Let us proceed now to the study of rapid playing.

—Are you going to give me exercises for achieving this?

—Here is the one and only exercise. Play the chord C-E-G-C, at the same time thinking of your fingers as four pillars. Now can you tell me if there exists a more rapid way of playing those four notes than by playing them as a chord, that is to say, together?

The young man looked at his master as if the latter were making fun of him. Finally he collected himself and said:

—All the same, that would be a little too simple! The idea of playing fast without effort throws me. Everyone knows that speed is not obtained without effort.

—Considering your response, I have no further need of explaining to you the secret of speed; you will discover it yourself, after two pieces of advice that I will give you. While keeping the feeling that each pillar is a separate support, you are going to play a rapid passage joining the notes at first into chords; then you are going to arpeggiate the chord while playing slower and slower. You work thus not for the *independence* of the fingers, but for their *isolation*. When after that you re-play the passage, isolate each finger one at a time. Then, re-play the chord, and little by little you will begin to understand that there is no chord, but an ensemble of independent sounds.

The student listened attentively and then interrupted the master:

—And to think that we are taught to *thump out* the chords!

—I share your legitimate indignation. Therefore it is understood you will practice your 16th Prelude by aligning as many notes as possible, at first felt as a chord. Even when you have to pass the thumb under the hand, hold the preceding note with the hand in a collected position. As for the octaves in the left hand, consider each one as being initial, while placing it independently of the preceding one; the awareness of interval between the consecutive octaves will come later. Do not think about lateral movements but maintain the thought that the piano keys are placed in the direction of the body; apply a well-syncopated bounce, with the hand forward into the keys towards the dropboard. You will see that even the idea of the octave will disappear and that it separates itself into two voices. I leave you to work on this premise, asking you at the same time not to allow your attention to become too fixed, but to do everything conscientiously and above all, with disengagement and ease.

I.

When a pianist who is in possession of an excellent technique and has already given several concerts, resolves to consult a master in order to revise and renew his playing, he opens the way towards ultimate perfection. Such courage which is a kind of self-effacement with regard to his work, is given only to a few rare artists. Many of our virtuosos content themselves with their acquired technique and thus limit their means of interpretation. Within their circle of ideas, nothing counts save their own point of view; they listen only to the voice which speaks within themselves; they know only their own artistic physiognomy which they imagine to be perfect. They often make us think of the tenor who, according to Huysmans "mirrors his vanity in the burst of his high C."

Now "the superior man," says Ernest Hello, "always finds his work unfinished; he struggles first, and succeeds later. The mediocre man is full of his own self. He does not struggle, but if he manages to succeed at first, he fails later."

One may therefore rejoice when a gifted young man, perceiving his imperfections and sensing his momentary limitations, bows to the knowledge which others have acquired. As an example of this will to search, we present in the following lessons the picture of a young pianist who respects himself and his work; the author of these pages, who assumes the role of professor, takes no credit. Our professor does nothing but return to the theses which others before him have formulated, adding his own experiences and making the deductions which impose themselves.

The fact that we refer to the grand school of piano playing arises from the importance of the theses themselves, and if sometimes the tone of our assertions becomes involuntarily authoritarian, it is owing to the convictions of those who, having found before us the truths which rule piano playing, have proved them during this grand epoch of the piano.

We invite the reader to be present in this spirit, at the lessons which follow.

* * *

The meeting between one who desires to learn new things, and another who can communicate them must be impregnated with complete objectivity. In this atmosphere the first conversation opened.

After the usual introductions, the young pianist explained:

—I have already given quite a few concerts, but I often have the feeling of not playing with perfect freedom. I do not refer to the burden of uncertainty when one floats between stage fright and over-boldness, but of the fact that for me a concert prevents the full realization of my usual playing.

—Stage-fright is only the fear of having it. In knowing this, one can avoid it. It is a question of re-educating oneself. Observe two people who are introduced; quite often each one is thinking solely of the impression he has made, instead of seeing "who" faces him. This is the first mistake which makes one lose confidence in himself. But you speak of another constraint which touches art directly. If you have something to say and you feel a desire of communicating it to the public, you were born to make yourself heard; all other motives for giving concerts have no reason for being.

—There is indeed in me, as you define it, a desire to make myself heard, since I feel I have something to say. But it is in the technical realization that things do not go as I would like them to.

—You think that it is in technique alone that one must seek liberty of execution? You will see that there exists a technique within the score, and in the end one finds it.

—Do you mean that each composer requires a particular technique?

—No; for the piano there is only one single technique which, if complete, adapts itself as naturally to the work of Beethoven as to that of Mozart. I affirm, also, that all masterworks point the way to a single and unique technique. This latter contains all of the touches, all of the most varied subtleties of expression. The day when you have mastered this power of realization you will see the rapport between the thought which the works contain and the gesture which that content commands.

—Then you do not separate music from technique in any way?

—This separation, so often commended, is the great misery of many musicians. This is what gives birth to those so-called techniques which should concern acrobats only. And from it also is born that feeling of inadequacy to express what one wants to say, which is the test of any interpreter; that inability you just now say is one of your troubles. Liszt has been reproached for having written technical acrobatics; but when one studies the musical sense which is at the source of his compositions, one plays them otherwise and there is no longer any question of that empty velocity which serves to impress a naive public.

" Great interpretation teaches us that all technique is included in the work itself. All that I can show you in the area of technique is nothing

other than the manifestation of actions which are conceptually present in the work. Not only in *a* work, but in all works which are truly conceived for our instrument. Every idea already carries within itself the rudiment of its manifestation. The will to manifest itself engenders the gesture which the idea requires for its realization.

—Could you give me an example?

—Do you play the Sonata in B minor of Liszt, the Sonata op. 111 of Beethoven, and that in B flat minor, op. 35, by Chopin?

—Yes, but a long time ago. I would like to study them again.

—Let us direct our attention for a moment to the diminished seventh which is the characteristic interval of these three works. In each of the Sonatas, this interval is in octaves; with Liszt in double octaves. Beethoven demands an execution so brilliant that some pianists must resort to the use of both hands.

—That way is of course not beethovian.

—Your answer touches the core of the problem. Cling to this truth: any gesture becomes natural when one understands the intention of the composer, the feeling he wants to express. It is less important at this moment if Beethoven had a notion of the manner of execution; I simply maintain the fact that the execution is conceived through the music. The treatment of this diminished seventh interval differs between Liszt and Chopin. The long curve which opens Chopin's Sonata in B flat minor and which is repeated in the development is carried by the entire brachial apparatus; the phrase takes an astonishing direction first of all in shifting from the thumb in the first octave [D flat], to arrive in the bass on the fifth finger for the second octave [E natural]. Liszt introduces this same leap, but to the treble with double octaves, in the ninth measure of his B minor Sonata. Does not this grand gesture of the whole arm-and-shoulder reflect the content of these masterworks? I do not wish to confine my thesis to only a few examples. The point is that these three executions are based on the same principle.

—I realize now that it is necessary to examine this principle in more detail.

—Certainly, but for the moment simply observe the relation between the music and its technical execution. After that we will proceed to the realization by applying it to your playing. What do you want to play for me?

The pianist played Busoni's transcription for piano of Bach's Organ Fugue in D major.

—What do you think of it?

—That it will be very interesting if together we inspect this work in order to arrive at a synthesis of its musical content and the execution which projects it. Let us isolate for a moment the technical problems which it presents, and go immediately to the heart of the problem. I want to illustrate to you an application of three different manners in which the arm can fall. Will you please stand up, and first, reach out horizontally with the full length of both arms . . . Now let them fall freely to the thighs.

" Well done. Now the right arm only, front-wise, extended and elongated straight out from the shoulder; let fall so that the mass of your arm bypasses your body without touching it . . . Already I observe that your drop is less free, therefore you do not completely relax the elevating force in your back.

" And now without bending the elbow, extend the stretched arm across the front of the body; then let the arm fall freely on the bias without your body being touched . . .

—Now the arm drops with difficulty.

—It should not be so. In all playing, here is something most simple, but which is all the more important. It is a lack of freedom that spoiled your octaves in the right hand when you played them in the bass at the end of the Fugue. It is therefore necessary to acquire this total freedom of descent when the arms are crossed. If you commence the First Etude, op. 10, no. 1, of Chopin with this lack, you are tense from the start and the same blockage will be present in all of your playing. In order to have a good supple gesture it is necessary to be conscious of the space which surrounds it, and to have a very close and reciprocal relationship with the underlying idea which directs the gesture.

—In sum you are saying that the mind governs the gesture in the act of piano playing as well as elsewhere, and it is upon this precept that your definition of technique is founded.

—Let us not go too fast and say for the moment that I define the *suppleness* of the technique, since any movement performed with an exaggerated contraction is blind and insensible to the space around it. Also, such playing does not "breathe." Moreover, each muscle needs to breathe as does the lung which regenerates the blood by renewing its oxygen. The muscle renews its forces through relaxation [détente]; now *the détente is the first condition of the free fall.*

—This constraint which keeps us from playing freely would therefore originate from the opposition of two actions.

—Exactly. To hold the forearm above the keyboard with the elbow, which neutralizes its weight, and then to keep moving the suspended

fingers in empty space to attack the keys, is to oppose the simplest physical laws.

" I go even further. To liberate yourself from all the exercises which preoccupy tens of thousands of pianists, know that they are more harmful than useful. Take a simple example: the theme of the Fugue that you just played: D E F# E, D E F# E, etc. If one uses these three notes, going and returning, as a result of a pure and simple three-finger exercise, the theme sounds as if played by an automaton, and in aping the automaton you have stiffened your organism. If I dare say, the trajectory of your fingers will be hung up by directives formulated in advance. The space around the movement of the playing will not be attained by repeating this sequence ad infinitum. You are acquainted with the Sonata op. 27, no. 2, the so-called *Moonlight,* of Beethoven. This Sonata, beat to death like no other, contains some marvelous things. In the execution, the triplets of the first movement have little by little lost their significance. Through a false technique, which consists in being regular and dynamically equal, the triplets become mechanical and dead. Phrase by lightly joining the last note of a triplet with the first note of the following triplet and tell me what you hear.

—They become linked in a continuous turning, rather than separated into groups of three.

—Continue playing in this manner the measures which follow the first exposition of the theme and listen solely to the movement of the triplets.

—It is as if the sky were turning above us.

—And the theme of the Fugue that you just played? One must see in this lively return to the D, the same turning-over as that of the triplets in the Sonata. Do you think that Bach was amusing himself by writing notes as for a children's game, four times the same figure followed by three beats of rest? How ridiculous this amusement if that were the only thing that Bach wanted us to hear. It would have quite the air of a senile game . . .

—I listen to what you are telling me about the theme of the Fugue.

—You remember what Chopin said: "Music which does not contain an idea is not music." And this theme turning round and round? Do you know any fugue in music literature that begins with an exposition as simple, which is developed in so gigantic a manner, up to the end? Is not this simple beginning isolated purposely by the three beats of rest which establish an expectation? I remember an old gravure reproduced in a work on Plato: an allegorical personage tries to open a trap in the cupola of the firmament in order to be able to observe from the outside the wheels of the universe.

—One question remains to be resolved; a technique inspired by ideas sometimes requires, I assume, a kind of "rubbing off the rust" obtained by the most elementary exercises for the fingers?

—Without contradicting the fact that every movement is the expression of an idea, even with infants, there does indeed remain for us the simple exercise, preparatory let us say.

—That is precisely a point I want to clarify with you, for I understand from your writings that you advocate a playing based on the springs of the flexors.

—And you have applied it well; it was obvious to me in your *non-legato* playing just a while ago.

—Do you consequently completely rule out raising of the fingers by means of the extensors?

—I do not totally exclude any muscular action. It serves to exercise certain muscles that are not made use of when we play. Playing achieved purely by lifting the fingers is condemned per se, but one must know why. Clark's text gives Liszt's explanation of this, but it can also be expressed in other ways.

" To raise a finger in order to strike a piano key may seem at first the necessary requirement for piano playing. But what appears logical in theory may often prove false in practice. Repeat this simple movement; you will see that it becomes fatiguing and that you have recourse to other means for the power to continue it. Here is a simple example of the way in which intelligence skirts the difficulty without battling against it. The rigidity of systems creates opposition; in the same way individuality will never understand universality.

" Let us summarize what we have observed today. Some reflections on the composition and its technical execution; the relationship between them. I have helped you to discover a deficiency in freedom of the fall when the arm finds itself in different positions. You have realized the importance of it in the execution of this work and in all technique.

" We have hereby prepared our next lesson, when I will treat *in detail* the work that you have just played, by demonstrating to you how one builds with the free fall as foundation, a synthesis of the three principal movements of our technique.

" Today I take leave of you with a single piece of advice. There is in your playing much more than is emerging at present. Please continue the same kind of work on the Prelude and Fugue that you have been doing, only listen to your playing differently; in particular, that your ear follows each sound. To do this effectively one must consider that the sound has three phases: its birth, its duration and its evanescence. With

most musicians, the impact of the initial sound obliterates all observation of the second phase, consequently they rarely catch sound of the last, the evanescence. It is therefore necessary to exercise the ear to immediately listen without contraction to the sound that is produced, and to follow it all the way through.

—What do you mean by "listening without contraction"?

—Preoccupation with the execution often prevents one from hearing what one is doing. The tension of execution then communicates itself to the whole organism and first of all to the ear. It is contraction of the ear which impedes hearing and which causes one to listen seldom, or poorly. It can even be said that many musicians play in a torpor that renders them deaf. This is of prime importance; any technique which by reason of the effort it exacts, blocks the ear, is obviously to be rejected; a technique which by its ease can be guided by the delight of listening, becomes the only good one. Do you now behold in this world of sound an ensemble of performance plus enjoyment? It is in this sense that I ask you to practice again this majestic work: Prelude and Fugue in D major of Bach-Busoni.

—Do you thus direct each one of your students toward the results of his own findings?

—My friend, know that one of the privileges given a possessor of great wealth is to watch others in the midst of their own joy of discovery, knowing that they too can be rewarded with the same riches.

II.

On the day of his second lesson the young pianist returned, full of warmth and enthusiasm. He had yet displayed only a part of his playing and moreover he had been presented with new ideas, most of which had not yet been explained. This trial period which he had willingly accepted had acted as a stimulant.

He seated himself at the piano and played again the same Prelude and Fugue of Bach-Busoni. The introduction which extends over two pages preceding the Prelude, sounded like a tranquil and powerful essay for the instrument. There was in this playing at once a sending towards space, reminiscent of the expansive resonance around the playing of an organ.

The young man gave each sound and each sonorous mass the time to develop and his playing thus became a veritable reflection of the great organ playing that one sometimes hears in churches when the organist respects the appropriate silences. The Prelude opens out by an active movement, supported at the beginning by the bass which one finds again

in the Ninth Symphony of Beethoven when the choir rises an octave higher, expressing joy of "millions of beings." Farther on the *non-legato* of the left hand allows a total freedom of singing to the right hand. Then the united parts of the two hands, superimposing the themes up to the highest note of the last of the two scales, express to the ultimate degree the incandescent joy of this Prelude, up to the moment when a sudden *piano* in the middle register comes to cut short this joy and a "*quasi-recitativo*" suggests the shadows of an infinite sadness, a reminder of the "Passion according to St. Matthew," which brings the Prelude to a close. The short silence between the Prelude and the Fugue is observed; then this last begins with a surprising turn-around of four *legato* notes, followed by the theme, a descending line in a continuous *non-legato.* Twice in this long Fugue a song travels through this whirling universe.

When the final note was played there was a silence; and wishing to prolong it, the professor signaled to the young pianist to remain quiet. It was only after several seconds that he spoke.

—You have played well; one proof is that the silence after the end was true, without a trace of confused noise as so often remains after execution of works of such broad scope.

—I felt very much at ease by calmly listening to what I was playing as though from a distance; but I am certain that you will have some observations to make.

—The observations will be your own once I shall have helped you to understand the synthesis of the act of playing. Here are the *givens.*

" You are acquainted with the principle of free fall of the arm; then the entrance into sound as the shock of the fall is lightened by the muscles of the back;[94] then the bounce from the line of arrest at the bottom of the depressed keys, which constitutes the table of playing.

—I know the theory in its general outlines, but without a doubt it contains much that needs further explanation.

—At this point we start with the bounce. For ease of execution, I evoke for each pianist the picture of a contrivance consisting of one or several narrow metal bands, firm but flexible, resembling piano keys, nailed down to the edge of a table and projecting out from it about 15 centimeters. This device can quickly acquaint us with the possibilities of flexibility and elasticity necessary for effecting the movement of bounce and of rebounding. These bands may be likened to a diving board, which

---

[94]See Chapter Four, (page 65.) "The bird, following a dizzying descent, places himself lightly on the ground. He accomplishes this by spreading out his wings just before he lands. He thus makes a cushion of air which protects him against too brutal a shock . . . . . ."

gives the diver his spring. Do not be carried away by this simile, since the case of the diver's bounce, whose weight is not at all confined, is of course different from that of the pianist whose arm is attached to the shoulder. The procedure for the pianists' exercise is first of all to test the flexibility at the end of the metal band with one finger, while the arm is outstretched and elongated. The extended arm, which remains passive, will spring up without the elevating force of the back intervening. If one repeats this maneuver while each time approaching closer to the edge of the table, the brachial apparatus has a tendency to replace, by a muscular action, that of the metallic spring. Finally, when one places the finger on the edge of the table itself he realizes that the bounce can no longer be achieved except by the organism. The metallic spring will have therefore communicated its functioning to the living organism of the brachial apparatus. To return to the piano keyboard, be sure to understand that the weak force which allows the key to rise when the finger releases it, furnishes no aid to the bounce; this is achieved purely by a reactive force of the brachial apparatus from the table of playing at the bottom of the keyboard.

—All of this is clear, but I would like to see its practical application to the playing itself.

—Consider the combination of movements which must operate almost simultaneously in the hand, the forearm and the arm. For a complete understanding it is necessary to have a clear idea of the flexibility of rotation during the descent. A piano key obviously always depresses vertically, whichever direction the hand takes, perpendicular or oblique. If a finger, seconded by the hand thrusts down vertically, control will become more difficult as speed increases. But the finger, hand and arm may launch a movement which, departing from the ivory, redescends in a curve. Then the descending course which the hand follows will be considerably longer than the actual distance to the key, at least twice as far. This long curve can be controlled during its flight to the key. It is possible to accelerate or decelerate the motion. In short, the *Wirbel-Impuls* (turning on an axis) is nothing other than the use of a long trajectory which joins a rectilinear distance of 10 millimeters at its target. This trajectory sustains the accelerations and decelerations of speed which are determined by the initial take-off of the gyration. It also becomes the regulator of the straight-line descent to the key. It will be the same in very rapid playing; the control exerted over the long curve permits infinite nuances in the attack which shapes the sound. You surely understand what an invaluable factor the light hand is to this action. It allows one to obtain, through the rotating gesture, a command which could not be achieved by a heavy hand. This is obviously very far removed from a habit of playing with raised fingers in order to produce sound.

—I am thinking of the steam engine whose pistons have two arrests and of the turbine with uninterrupted movement.

—After these reflections one can get a precise idea of the causes which provoke a hard and short sound and those that create the long and mellow sound. What happens when one strikes the ivory violently? First the shank of the hammer is shaken in every direction and consequently it vibrates laterally; the hammer rubs the string instead of striking it in a straightforward manner; result, the strident sound.

" Let us look more closely at the faculties and functioning of a string. Its possibility of tension depends on the elasticity and resistance of its material. To obtain the maximum, it is necessary that the amplitude of its vibrations do not go beyond its intrinsic capacities. In forcing beyond these capacities one alters the vibration or breaks the string. Now, if by too violent a shock one forces its elasticity by so going beyond the limits of its normal vibrations, the string reacts as does a living thing; it shrinks immediately its action, the vibrations become instantaneously less ample and the sound diminishes very soon. If on the contrary one eliminates the shock by accelerating only progressively the speed of the hammer, the string functions normally within its limits; the sonorous effect will be long, mellow, and as powerful as one will wish.

—Exertion of pressure after a violent shock is equivalent therefore to wiping out the action after having killed the living sound.

—I like your definition very much. You understand the importance in this erroneous idea of those who believe that only strength can do justice to their "temperament."

—It is, of course, a psychological error.

—It is indeed that, but what is the consequence? Under the shock of the brutal blow the action of the hammers escapes from all control, and one develops the habit of pressing strongly on the already depressed key which then remains immobile. On the other hand, the lightening of the hand permits the key to rise again, a millimeter, so that the hammer draws closer to the string without touching it. What effect, difficult to understand, does this then have on the string? It so happens that the sound is amplified, stays no longer shut up within the instrument, but renewed, it takes flight towards space. This manner of lightening the hand is rapidly acquired if one is not too preoccupied with the actual striking of each note. It is a question here of general lightening which soon becomes a habit. Later this habit will allow such application to each key separately.

—You make a distinction therefore in the act of playing, between the movement of depressing the key and that of releasing it?

—Yes, but they are again combined in the movement of gyration. It is up to you now to "live" these gestures. After having given you an idea of what I call "the pursuit in the playing"—term borrowed from the technique of the piano—I return to the descent of the key. Here is the process in three phases: a) the contact without shock with the ivory; b) the accelerated descent under the effect of the gyratory movement; c) the reception at the bottom of the key, followed by a gyratory bounce. During this last phase, the last millimeters before reaching the table of playing is measured by *the hand which pre-feels* and which contributes, by means of that, to the dosage of the dorsal action.

—What do you mean by "pre-feel"?

—The subtle faculty of the digital sensibility is quickened by the sensitivity of the ear which regulates the subsequent action. Now, I repeat, to be able to listen without contraction is the concern of some three thousand internal hair cells which are found in the ear. I will return to this at the end of this lesson. First we finish the problem of the physical action. If one designates as element *A* the free fall and the bounce, there remain two other *givens* for us to study in order to complete the circle of the synthesis. The aspect of the keyboard constitutes element *B*. Look at the form of the keys. The whites are to the eye a lengthwise total of 15 cm., that of the narrow part being 10 cm. and that of the part closest to the edge being 5 cm., while the breadth at this place is 22 mm. The black key has a length of 9 cm. and a width of 1 cm. Viewing this assemblage, the general impression which strikes one is that of an array of white and black keys spreading out laterally. But the keys deserve to be considered in another sense which is far more important to the playing. Departing from the shank of the hammer, the direction of the keys is completely towards the pianist. The importance of this fact leaps to the eyes if one realizes that a simple scale is composed of a chain reaction upon these strips which at first exhibit their length of 15 cm., and only after that their breadth of 22 mm. If one examines a white key for a moment it is apparent that its width of 22mm. does not furnish the same sureness to the touch as does its total length, which is 50 mm. from the shank of the hammer to the edge. The aviator coming in for a landing judges his point of contact with the ground and calculates the trajectory of his descent in relation to the length of the landing strip. Apply this to the piano and one can say that the finger executes in the vertical plane a short trajectory which terminates at the desired landing point. Upon arrival the finger becomes a sort of prolongation of the key.

—But in Clark's text, does not Liszt speak in terms that condemn the prolongation of the mechanism?

—No, he does not refer to this kind of prolongation of a key, but of "imitation of the mechanical action of the hammers." You are right to alert me to such a possible error in interpretation. If this new approach to the direction of the keys is considered, one clearly sees that the suspended bridge created by the arm following the free fall becomes completely the prolongation of the keys. It is also clear that the finger which serves as a pillar of the bridge draws the key in the direction of the body. The natural adherence prevents the finger from sliding off the keyboard and permits the fingers to crawl in order to recover the lost ground. But here is where the final element *C* is added to elements *A* and *B*. This element *C* is the pronation, the movement having its origin in the back, which expands the shoulders and which serves to tip *en dédans*[95] the entire ensemble of arm, hand and fingers. Incorporation of this pronation remains still in the lengthwise direction of the piano keys (resembling the use of a rake), and the two combined actions reach their goal through the free fall and the bounce. Therefore, the act of playing becomes the result of three movements which are three-dimensional in direction.

—What means do you advocate for achievement?

—It is very simple; here is an excellent example in Chopin's Etude, op. 10, no. 1. Assume largely an attitude of pronation and begin at the top of the descending arpeggios in the second measure. You arrive in the bass, meanwhile having turned *en dédans,* always with the whole arm and shoulder, on the E of this measure; you now exert a slight pull on this E and then you bounce lightly with the aid of the back to play the next note, and in the same fashion those that follow; when ascending you make the same muscular turn, always *en dédans.*

" And here I return to the authority of the ear. The action prescribed above can be perfected only if you listen to the sonority of each tone. The hearing can attain such a degree of virtuosity that one can hear a sound, then put this perception into a soft tone in order to re-hear once more its full volume. The greater your ease of hearing the duration of the sound, the more supple will become the action towards the following note. By working in this fashion, this First Etude of Chopin will very quickly be transformed from an exercise of separate notes to a melody. It is the succession of intervals which makes this Etude one of the most powerful and at the same time one of the most beautiful works for the piano. If, on the contrary, you attempt to thoroughly master this Etude by practicing it solely for accuracy of the free fall at a distance from the keys, I can guarantee that after five years it will still present the same difficulties.

---

[95]See nomenclature (page 57.)

—In your estimation then, good playing depends on perfection in listening to oneself.

—On condition that the action does not conflict with the laws of nature; further that it does not conflict with a free and, by consequence, natural perception of the ear.

" A tone which sounds in space is quite another thing from a note inscribed on paper. The reproduction which demands that it be faithful only to the printed work is nonsense. Counterpoint exists only on paper for in space the voices cross but never touch, as they do in the writing. The sonorous tone enters relativity as is proper for all movement in space. While practicing, listen to the sound in space and become conscious of your movements and gestures within this same space. The greatness of Liszt's playing rests in the fact that he directed all of it toward a vast cosmic idea, one which coincided through this excellence with all conceptions of grandeur in music. At our next lesson, we will enter into certain details concerning the consequences of what I have said today.

—It is quite Liszt's thesis when he says "The supreme harmony of the Cosmos is reflected in the harmony of the spirit."

—You will be rewarded in other respects for your enthusiasm. Once an individual has a clear glimpse of this grand outline, who can tell where he may leap? In your interest, and to best evaluate this thesis, review the first and the last of the twenty-four Chopin Etudes. I will return next time to these two Etudes.

III.

At his third lesson, the young pianist was greeted with the following words:

—I am perhaps more curious to know your reactions, without a doubt more lively at present than when you first came to listen to my explications regarding a kind of playing which interested you. Do you make any progress with this group of ideas which I have sketched for you in their broadest outlines?

—I read a word in one of your previous books; today I have grasped the full significance of it.

—A little book written a decade ago?

—Yes, *La musique et l'artisan du piano.*[96] You quote there a statement of Archimedes: "Give me a fulcrum and I will lift the earth." That famous

---

[96]Paul Roës. Henry Lemoine & Co., Paris, 1939.

imaginary fulcrum in the sidereal world of which the illustrious geometer spoke is quite simply the *essential point* in the method you have explained to me. But do you look beyond the simple idea of a physical fulcrum?

—At the beginning, it is on the physical plane of technique that the idea strikes you, but soon another meaning is revealed. You have understood that every act stems from an idea and that the correctness and the worth of the act depends on the value of the idea.

—If one ponders on this cascade of consequences, one truly wants to retire into this vast domain to which so few people will accede.

—Stay with your work while not isolating yourself from the world; indeed be very prudent about this, for what people will not forgive is that you do not mingle with them. I will, rather, remind you of your own words: "I have something to say to them." Let us then take up where we left off last time. Does the physical fulcrum become a reality in your playing? Let me insist on this point today; we shall have plenty of opportunities to develop the other ideas. I recommended that you study slowly Chopin's First Etude, but starting on the second measure. Well now, what exactly have you felt while developing it according to the principle of the triple movement?

—That every action becomes, by itself, rotative in the sense of which Liszt spoke.

—His *Wirbel-Impuls* imposes itself quite naturally. Do me the pleasure of playing the Etude in question without going beyond your newly acquired possibilities.

After playing, the young pianist asked a question:

—Do you consider the rising line of the arpeggios as an anacrusis and the E in the treble as the strong beat?

—Why this question?

—Because in so doing a melody is released that one never hears . . . Putting a strong beat on the E at the beginning of the second measure, I have a tendency to make a long phrasing of four beats in which two groups of 16th notes represent one beat; and thus the bass notes in the fifth measure, becoming quarter notes, singularly reinforce the idea of an anacrusis calling for a strong beat.[97]

---

[97]*Ed. note:* Marie Stuart de Backer adds: "I have Roës' copy of the Chopin Studies. He here divides a measure in two, that is to say in groups of eight 16th notes, with an accent on the top E, obtaining thus, 4 beats in 2 measures starting from the beginning. He places a kind of anacrusis on the 4th beat of this division, that is to say on the beginning of the second half of each second bar. Roës often asked for a slight accent on the 4th beat (or the 3rd if the last) in any measure."

—I see that it is not in vain that I asked you to commence this Etude on the second measure; you have perceived that pronation begun on the fifth finger completely changes the aspect of the Etude.

—And with this the fingering of the right hand, which is constantly extended with the fifth on the high note and the thumb on the low note of each group of 16th notes, becomes self-explanatory and the difficulties disappear.

—I have seen and heard this in your execution, only you still are making too much demonstration of the pronation. The movement is still too visible and it will take you some time to "lodge" all action within the over-all flexibility of the organism. Liszt sometimes made a remark which never failed to annoy certain of his students. One day while explaining the rotary motion, he suggested to one of them that he should not make "omelets." By that he meant, once and for all, that "lovely gestures" have the faculty of pleasing, but in reality are parasites of the playing, while the true technique reposes strictly on the inner impulsion.

—I well understand. I will try to find the necessary suppleness in the high arch by extending the hand through its pillars, the fingers . . .

— . . . at the same time continuing this movement in the brachial apparatus. Now let us press on further. Half of the playing is done by the fingers which are playing, but there is the other half of playing which is as important to understand, that is to say, the fingers which are not playing. I am not a partisan of rendering the fingers independent; I think rather of the isolation of the fingers. The slightest crispation or contraction of one single finger which is not playing can interfere with action of the playing finger. This second aspect of playing is generally neglected.

" It works both ways; if the crispation of a non-playing finger provokes a stiffness in its playing neighbor, reciprocally, contraction of a playing finger stiffens its neighbor in repose.

" In order to free the action it is necessary to disengage from the playing those fingers which are not participating. If a passage presents difficulties, the cause of it is most often found in the non-playing fingers.

" Ease in playing octaves is obtained by relaxing the three fingers in the middle, which, by their non-activity, follow the spring of the octaves. One could compare their function to that of the kangaroo's tail which directs his spring when leaping contrarily. When the middle fingers are active, in a chord for example, they maintain, nay, dominate the thumb and fifth finger. The secret of the utilization of activity and non-activity of the fingers depends on the relative dosage of decontraction required.

" What I have just said should aid you in the execution of the First Chopin Etude, for the great stretches found there often provoke contractions.

—What facilitates enormously the execution of that work is pressing down the concentration of lower back muscles against the chair, which makes my hands light.

—Concerning this pressing down, I want to add this: you can, if you are supple, draw the left shoulder-blade downwards and through this movement involve the mass of the left arm. This effort will lighten the right side of the body so that, with the Etude in question, the bass will be heavy and powerful; and by means of this the arpeggios in the right hand will be played in a totally free manner.

—It appears to you thus, that one transfers the weight from the left side to the right side and vice versa?

—Which at the same time interchanges the lightness of the hands. In connection with this alternation for use of forces either in the right or left side of the back muscles, there is a matter of the chair to consider. One of the centers in the great forces of our body resides in the region of the pelvis. By drawing downwards either of the shoulder blades, one is aware that this muscular mass becomes concentrated on the pelvis, giving the sensation of being heavily seated. The flexible placing of this body position is important; it influences the liberty of contraction and of de-contraction of the back and of the whole brachial apparatus. These conditions also apply to violinists.

" When one day a young aspirant-pupil announced himself to Marsick, the latter asked him to stand up, body straight, in a natural way. "Do you feel at ease standing up, does your body rest well on the pelvis? No? . . . you do not feel it? . . . Come back and see me when you have achieved this."

" For the pianist, the importance of the liberation of his superstructure through this concentration of weight on the pelvic area, becomes also imperative. Would you please look at my chair and tell me what you see.

—The back is very lightly curved outwards from the foot to the top; it invites support for the lower part of the back, leaving the upper part as well as the shoulder blades free.

—Yes, vertically the chair back is lightly curved towards the rear; crosswise it is straight and not hollowed as in most chairs which interfere with lateral displacement. You see, also, strong traces of usage on the varnish of the dowels at the bottom of the chair back, while toward the top the varnish has remained intact. Here is the lesson in concrete example, in the wearing of my chair.

—It is very expressive, indeed it represents decades of work . . . You condemn therefore the bench and the stool?

—They have the inconvenience of constraining forces which, on the contrary, with a good chair having a back, are free. This brings us back to the decontraction of a part of our organism, for example, the fingers. A good deal depends on the quality of the muscles, of their sensitivity, of the rapidity of their action and reaction. To clarify this phenomenon for you, observe the first Prelude and the last Etude of Chopin. In each of these the thumb of the right hand plays the melody. And in these same two compositions the second finger must follow instantaneously. To make *cantabile* the melody played by the thumb, and at the same time to get the index finger to descend immediately without one of these fingers being influenced by the other, is one of the clues to Chopin's and Liszt's playing. The latter, even more than Chopin, used a fingering of successive thumbs in the rapid passages; this because of his ability to disengage the non-active index finger.

—How can one acquire what you term isolation of the fingers?

—By first playing simultaneously notes of a passage as if they constituted a chord, then by arpeggiating more and more slowly, while isolating each finger turn by turn. A key-exercise is found in Chopin's Etude op. 25, no. 5. While you play the *appoggiatura,* lightly pull on the key, from an extended arm position, and lean with your fingers on the chord; but beforehand play the chord not in a block, but in feeling the fingers as isolated pillars. And thus, I arrive automatically at the execution of the trill and the tremolo. Let us take as preparatory exercise the first of the Paganini-Liszt Etudes, in G minor. After the opening scale, we find entire pages which cannot be executed except by pronation. The tremolos are all directed towards the index finger. I advise you to play throughout with the second finger slightly in advance, as if the fifth finger had to play a "grace note." Little by little the index finger will descend with ease while the melody is maintained by the thumb. The necessity for pronation is so evident in this study that I have often thought that if Liszt had not discovered his *Wirbel-Impuls* through his creative imagination, he would have learned it from Paganini through his image of the violin bow in high position, which obliges one to make an inward motion with the arm. It will be easy for you to consider the trill or the tremolo as a series of appoggiaturas in which the note values will be equal. The phrasing will develop itself, through the direction of pronation. Begin a trill or tremolo slowly, and once it takes form, divide it into triplets, then into eighths and into sixteenth notes.

—You consider then the trill and the tremolo as a static effect, which one hears first as a motif that will later be transformed into a theme . . .?

—Exactly, and considering it from this angle, one can say: there is no trill, these are motifs in a passage. The role of the ear is essential for the exercise and execution of the trill or tremolo; never play the succeeding note without the ear's having absorbed the note just played! After this great work of listening, the trill will emerge as if by magic. Do you recall the long trills in Chopin's Nocturnes and in Liszt's Sonata? In the last sonatas of Beethoven you will find abundant material. Already, with Beethoven, the trill takes the place of a melody; do not forget the entrance of the cuckoo's song in the *Pastoral* Symphony. There, the trill is slowly prepared and gradually accelerates. You will discover in the Sonata op. 53 the same execution for the tremoli of the first movement; pronation will render them easy and fluid. Next time, we will have a recapitulation of what you have studied, but from a different approach.

—You have referred to me a number of works that I want to review completely.

—Do this with composure and simplicity; do not criticize too much in detail, for example the descent of the key. Send it down with a gyratory movement and listen to the sound, because this will without fail adjust the following action. Our next meeting will be devoted to this subject.

IV.

—At this fourth lesson I want to mention a new fundamental element as well as other details. First a summary of elements we have together observed, plus some additional advice on these. This most condensed mass of substance which I have presented to you during three lessons must be assimilated calmly and viewed with perspective.

" Beginning with your first visit, you asked me to acquaint you with my ideas. I believe the time has come to take you back first of all to the technique of playing that you had already acquired; the best way seems to be that you play for me something which you know thoroughly. For the moment do not try to incorporate any new acquisitions.

—I will give you a work which I have played in concert, but I must tell you that some changes already impose themselves, for it is difficult for me to forget what I have since acquired.

—Forget is not the word. Each change, each adaptation in your playing requires time, and the more slowly this process is accomplished, the better it will succeed . . . Guard carefully against too rapid a changeover. What now seems to you imperative you have partially discovered for yourself, and this will preserve you from imitation. Use that as your base, without anticipating what will follow in its own time. Play therefore at your ease without too much reflection.

—I will play for you Chopin's Sonata in B flat minor.

His performance was that of a sonata recently practised again. He seemed totally surprised at the beautiful result.

—You give evidence that your playing has been simplified . . . also that it has gained in amplitude. Tell me, and will you please weigh your answer . . . to what point do you feel that your interpretation has changed?

—The work itself illustrates to me the truth of your ideas about the execution. What evidence may I say of the continuous importance of pronation! Thanks to it, how well the themes are projected to the ear in a different way!

—That is all I wanted you to know. You are realizing that another interpretation from what one ordinarily hears, is imposing itself. And the consequences . . . you do not fear controversies?

—I have no fear of an opinion which is the result of ignorance of principles contained within the works themselves.

—Now, if you will be seated in this easy chair, I will let you hear the three works you have played during the course of our lessons: the Prelude and Fugue in D major of Bach-Busoni, then the First and Twenty-fourth Etudes of Chopin, and I am going to add Chopin's Etude op. 10, no. 6, and *Il Penseroso* from the *Années de Pèlerinage en Italie* by Liszt. I have chosen these five pieces for the following reasons: I would like to demonstrate to you that in these different works the same technique can be applied, the same method be used. When Chopin spoke of his "blue note," that velvet and mellow tone which he sought while playing his improvisations, his nocturnes, his mazurkas or some of his preludes, this was in reality only an over-all adaptation of his method. It may seem at first contradictory that this method could be incorporated throughout all the works written for piano, in spite of different ideas that each one expresses. But consider the immense synthesis of Liszt, embracing all the manifestations of universal thought. For him, technique is based on the essence of music; everything springs from the same source. Each technical detail of the execution is an integral part of the broad interpretation.

—Just as one can construct dissimilar monuments using the same materials.

—Exactly. Would you therefore not only listen, but also look at the same time. You will see that the action remains the same, while you hear multiple nuances in the formation of the sound, in the *crescendi,* the *diminuendi,* and above all in the *rubato.*

" Try therefore to follow me in my playing, in the technique of my action, and for the moment lose consciousness of the mastery which you already possess, for this will allow you to listen better, and better to observe.

—It is a fact that most pianists who listen to another's performance hear, through the soloist, only themselves.

—Ah, my dear friend, knowing how to appreciate the playing of another represents a complete apprenticeship in objectivity. The most astounding musician in this direction was Rachmaninoff; he always stressed the merits of an interpreter which he had the knack of discovering. So many souls are prompted to criticize and so few . . . with any purpose.

—It is this objectivity which must have led Rachmaninoff to seek advice from Godowsky.

—You understand; now please listen to me.

When the last octaves, interrupted by silences, concluded *Il Penseroso,* the young man remained pensive for some moments. His absorption had been complete.

—What a store of knowledge remains still to be secured! . . . What beautiful perspective!

—Since we make a complete study, let us be practical. One could say that without an introductory explication of the method, you would have distinguished very little.

—I have no doubt. In this playing scarcely any movement is apparent, and one would say that there is magic concealed in its immobility.

—A playing which displays evidence of too many motions is one encumbered with parasites which destroy its intensity. Uselessly spectacular, it fools a too credulous public. We now tap the secrets concealed in this immobility. You were able to hear that each tone, even at the greatest speed, has its own time to develop. Immediately after the action of lowering the keys, let us say an eighth of the duration of the sound, the ear has time to impel the following action. I repeat, the ear is a regulator of our movements and at the same time the guide. It follows then that the ear learns to listen with the same proportion of serenity as the technical ability has attained. It is for this reason that one works slowly and not solely for exercising the fingers. It is necessary to achieve mastery of the ear. It may be slightly brutal to say, but most of our vituosos are deaf when they play. The physical effort corks their ears and they perform passages trusting only to be successful. Awareness of sound duration is by consequence determined through the training of the ear.

" You could notice that the lateral displacements of my hands are so rapid that this allows me, in the Prelude and Fugue for example, to play the variations of the themes, which are found sometimes in the treble, sometimes in the bass, a fraction of a second ahead of the beat. I say, parenthetically, that the lateral displacement can be the cause of a slight stiffness in the hands; this is produced when one does not retreat the origin of the action far enough towards the back. In general, as soon as the action has a tendency to approach the fingertips, the playing shrinks and slows down; this happens frequently in the playing of trills.

" To return to the anticipated descent [playing a fraction of a second ahead of the beat], we are bordering on the whole problem of continuity in playing. This anticipation, as I call it, is contrary to the musical notation. To reproduce exactly what has been written on the paper is incompatible with the space in which the music evolves. The playing would then have a mechanical precision which would not at all correspond with the phenomena of nature where nothing is absolutely simultaneous. But let us beware of any exaggeration in the anticipated action.

—The mechanical playing, the playing like a robot, has always appeared to me as the negation of music, and one does hear it, let us say . . . sometimes . . .

—Here you begin to touch on the problem of interior rhythm realized in space, something every great interpreter must possess.

" There also exists a natural tendency which provokes anticipation: the pronation. And now the crucial point. One has such a habit of hearing the notes with a certain delay that one fails to realize this fault. One often wonders why a work he is playing seems to halt inopportunely instead of continuing with facility. In the Etude op. 25, no. 3 of Chopin, the playing often seems to begin again at the start of each measure. To obtain a continuity, it simply suffices to anticipate the first two notes in quarter-note triplets of the first variation, in order to avoid an acceleration towards the end of each measure. In this action, the role of pronation is capital. I want to demonstrate this to you, by means of an actual photograph, how much this action is inherent in the natural disposition of the hand. Have you looked carefully at the hands of Liszt and Chopin?

—You mean the picture of Liszt's hand seen from the outside and that of Chopin's seen from the inner side?

—Yes; these two hands complement each other and they confirm the action of pronation. The hand of Liszt covers the thumb, which is the opposite of the thumb placing itself underneath the hand. It shows the logical result of the broad pronative movement which starts in the back. All the same, the chief factor in the action of pronation is not the thumb; on the contrary, it is the index and the third finger. And if you study

carefully the powerful implantation of the index finger in Chopin's hand, you will understand why these two photos complete each other.

" On the one side, by covering the thumb, one liberates the flexors of the other fingers; on the other side, the implantation of the index finger, so developed in Chopin, is the mark of the power of a flexor which is completely free and constantly in action. Here then is a new face to the problem of the anticipation provoked by pronation. You will find from now on in Liszt's and Chopin's works this element which will guide you, and the result will be an interpretation different from the one usually heard. But have you noticed anything else in my playing that interests you?

—I will tell you frankly, knowing that you can explain it to me. I have observed that, from time to time, you slide your fingers in the direction of the hammer shank instead of drawing the keys towards you.

—Here is the reason for it. You could see that I make this gesture only in the *dolce* or *pianissimo* passages. If one uses force to push towards the shank, the adherence of the fingers produces a harsh tone and the action is restricted. The great sonorous masses will have to be the result of a vertical movement or else drawing the fingers towards you, depending on the quality of timbre that you want to obtain. Think of the gesture of Liszt who, according to Clara Wieck, would draw himself down before the instrument when he played *forte.* But on the other hand, many an exquisite nuance is obtained by the action of sliding the fingers towards the shank; if one employs the elevating force of the back for this, the adherence loses its effect.

" *Rubato* is effected in either direction, but always while searching the long trajectory, by means of rotation.

—I did not know that adherence played so important a role.

—It is a phenomenon proper to our nature.

—I had never thought about it.

—Another thing on the technical side that you could see in the Etude op. 10, no. 6, is the readjusting of the balance within the hand itself. When the fifth finger plays the principal melody, it serves as a pivot; the other fingers move around it and can thus play the accompaniment which is in reality a secondary melody.

" And here is the new element that I announced to you at the beginning of this lesson. Its importance is as great as that of the *Wirbel-Impuls* because it is the complement of it. Have you noticed, in the Etude op. 10, no. 1, that the thumb of the right hand often has to play on a key that the thumb of the left hand is already holding down?

—Yes, and it seemed to me, in this Etude as well as in other pieces, to be a clumsy writing.

—On the contrary this element contains a stimulant for execution.

" This which you believe to be a blunder, as do many other pianists, appears in this Etude eleven times in the ascending passages and fourteen times in the descending passages. The C played by the thumb of the left hand would be for the right hand a dead note if it were not renewed in a different manner from that of the spelling; notice that Chopin wrote, in this Etude alone, *twenty-five times* this incommodity!

" You know by experience that the *Wirbel-Impuls* has its true impetus at the moment of rebound. Now, in the place where the thumb of the right hand has to re-play rapidly the C already depressed by the left hand, one can provoke what I shall call a *shaking*. This is a succession of ultra rapid actions, which alternate between the two arms; it is the synthesis of the rebound, of the anticipation and of the *Wirbel-Impuls*. This alternating movement is a new possibility of experiencing the relationship of the *action between the arms*. You will find numerous examples of it in the works for piano, among others in the Chaconne of Bach-Busoni where, at the twenty-ninth measure before the end, the A is successively repeated between the left and the right hand. The repeated action on this same A develops into a sort of tremolo between the two arms.

" To execute this movement, it is necessary to commence with a rebound which rises high enough, and to reduce little by little its trajectory. When you let fall both of the fully extended arms to just above the keys without depressing them, at the moment of arresting the fall, the body has a tendency to bend slightly forward. At this instant, the body loses its equilibrium a little, being drawn along by the falling mass, and one has the feeling that the contraction furnished by the elevating muscles of the back and shoulders has a slight tendency to be transferred to the forearm and wrist. But if you let fall one arm and at the same time raise the other, it produces a slow tremolo between the the two arms, what we might call a balancing between the weight of each arm, one which maintains the body in perfect equilibrium. The momentary jolt thus feels eased and less intense.

—Let me ask a question. Do you believe that it is lack of this balancing which causes so many pianists to lean forward?

—It is possible, but let us complete our study of this movement. We have verified that it permits the body to maintain its equilibrium, and in this way the musculature of the back becomes the element of union between the arms.

" It also gives the impression that the hands have become light, but this sensation, important as it may be, is not the only advantage which

this alternating displacement affords. You know that our thoughts, as well as our acts, depend on our faculty of comparison.[98] This process of comparison is in complete accord with the movement of which we speak, for this flexibility of equilibrium, where the back acts as a hinge between the right and left brachial apparatuses, demands a quick and intelligent exchange between our mental and physical capacities.

" You can ascertain that my hands continually change places, one in relation to the other, in an undulating movement and in opposing directions . . . Have you noticed? Well then, try it for yourself, first by playing the A flat major Polonaise of Chopin, and then in any other piece.

—. . . In the Polonaise this movement seems to me particularly effective, for one has the impression that one hand stimulates the action of the other.

—Now transpose this freedom to the Chopin Etude op. 25, no. 2, and you will see that this balancing is one that was written in. Study this alternating displacement in the Sonata "After a Reading of Dante" by Liszt, in the Second Paganini-Liszt Etude; apply the same action, but considerably reduced, to the *"legato"* passages of other pieces. In this playing particularly, the arrival at the key bed is almost simultaneous; if one seeks absolute simultaneity one must imitate the machine, a playing that is lifeless.

The young pianist appeared most curious.

—Just the opposite of what you say is taught; it is required that everything be made to sound strictly together, failing which, one sins against the first rule of playing.

—The rule of playing is determined by the artist; it is for him to judge whether non-simultaneity between the two hands enhances the music or renders it incoherent. It is not a matter of playing the melody ahead of the accompaniment, for the anticipation that I have reference to must be almost imperceptible.

" To end this lesson, I want to explain to you the end of the sentence in which Liszt declares: "A method which teaches one to strike, to fall, or to throw, is at fault for this alone, since it interrupts the magnetic flow and radiation from the central forces." The magnetic flow and radiation from the central forces are provoked by the sensitivity of the hand. With some experimenting, when you play an interval you will feel spreading up to and into the hand a force which originates in the musculature of the back. This irradiation, generated by the digital sensitivity,

[98]See Chapter Three, Sections III and V, faculty and process of comparison.

starts from the central organs and is propagated all the way up into the hand, when one uses the movement of pronation. When playing an octave it is necessary therefore to sensitize first the fifth finger and then the thumb, in such a manner that the keys are depressed simultaneously. This sensation, of which we become more and more conscious, soon becomes the true memory in the hand. Consequently, put your attention first to the exterior of the hand. To liven this irradiation, use the high-arched vault[99] which transmits the current of irradiation with the maximum of sensitivity. Thus, as Liszt expresses it, "the arms become fingers."

—I see the structure of all the elements of playing; pronation, bounce, *Wirbel-Impuls,* shaking, irradiation, all united in the magnetic flow of radiation from the central forces.

—At present let us proceed with the principles which we have examined. I want to give you one last directive for your daily work. You know perhaps that Chopin recommended that his pupils practice in *staccato?*

—Yes, but one generally understands the *staccato* as an attack directed towards the key!

—I know it, but it is not that action that he was thinking about, for that would be the contrary of the bounce. It is a question first of making contact with the ivory before beginning the ultra-rapid descent followed by a bounce no less rapid, without involving the wrist.

" This last will undergo a counter-balancing while all the time remaining motionless. The wrist remains passive. The action must be executed while holding the arm outstretched; thus, its launching is the work of the flexors, and the relaxation followed by a contraction, cause of the bounce, comes from the dorsal forces.

" The highly-arched vault spreads the fingers lightly and its supple movements take the place of an action consisting of raising and lowering the fingers. Now it is at this point the difficulty arises, that of bringing the fingers back to the keys in order to continue the *staccato.* Don't forget how a bird perches. To play a continued *staccato,* Busoni's advice is simple and effective: "It is not necessary that I hear the shock of your fingers on the ivory."

—Yes, but what is finally the means of arrival at the keys?

—The high-arched vault, because it is necessary to avoid the disastrous habit of raising the fingers. The playing must be directed from below upwards, not from above downwards. The approach must be delicate but rapid, the action which follows, quick as lightning. In *legato,* even with perfect liaison, there will remain always a latent *staccato* when played

---

[99]See nomenclature (page 59.)

as I have described it to you. You will obtain thus the clarity which a brilliant playing requires. Avoid curving the fingers too much and watch that the wrist and the elbow remain inactive.

" If you play *staccato* by taking advantage of the *Wirbel-Impuls,* you will notice—and this is one of the most important observations of our four lessons—that at the instant of launching, whatever finger is involved, the transverse axis of the hand is found vertically over the finger in action and is displaced laterally for the action of another finger. Thus the weight of the arm and of the hand is found always perpendicularly above the fingers which are playing; by means of this fact, the hand controls their functioning. Keep good control of this lateral displacement of the weight.

" Imagine, when the hand is displaced as much as an interval of a third, for example, that a plumb line is attached to the highest point of the vault formed by the hand. Then picture the line hanging lower than the keyboard, indicating the direction of the balance of weight. Each time that the hand is displaced laterally by any interval whatsoever, this imaginary plumb line is displaced in the same direction and must continue to hang vertically from the culminating point of the vault. Through this imaginary game you can control the solidity of the finger-pillars. You thus obtain an equal and very distinct sonority from each note of the interval.

" Maintaining this control is synonymous with "working slowly." Study in this way the First Etude of Chopin, where the distances between the notes present themselves as great gaps in the conformation.

" In resume, do not forget what Liszt taught us through his researches; return frequently to the source of technique in assuring yourself that your deductions are well-founded.

" Spread the hand lightly when you play, without the fingers losing their solidity as pillars. You will find by experience, in your musical career as in your whole life, that curved fingers betray pain and also egoism, and that the open hand indicates ease . . . and generosity.

" In concluding, I wish to draw your attention to that which dominates the whole of our lessons.

" Ardent as this research may be, do not limit yourself to exploring exclusively the domain of the piano. The power of our means of execution does not come from our work alone; the effectiveness of our efforts depends also upon our general culture. All our playing is but the reflection of what we are; true technique is nothing more than the manifestation of spiritual gifts. The lesson that Liszt has given to us is the most eloquent testimony of this.

FIN

Paris, August, 1954.

APPENDIX A. Frederick Horace Clark

American born in the year of 1860, the young pianist, Frederick Horace Clark, arrived in Europe at age sixteen; in Leipzig he studied with Dr. Oscar Paul. Following a return to the United States, "where he had good success as a teacher," his second European experience was in Berlin. After some study with Heinrich Ehrlich, Moritz Moszkowski and Oscar Raif, he was one of a group of students who "went over to Deppe." He met Anna Steiniger—a talented performer as well as one of Ludwig Deppe's assistant piano teachers—and, after not too long, married Anna. Together they established the "Clark-Steiniger system" based on careful study and observation of the various theories of piano technique that were developed during this period in Europe.

Subsequently the couple came to Boston and, after a time, to the Chicago area. After "the loss of the gifted Steiniger," Clark married one of his young pupils.

Clark returned to Berlin a few years before World War I, where he continued teaching until, as an American, he was no doubt obliged to emigrate to Switzerland in 1914. He died in Zürich in January of 1917.

He was author of several publications, written mostly in the German language and published in Germany. Any in the English language were apparently published in Chicago. Sometimes he wrote under the pseudonym of Leo St. Damian.

References for this material are as follows: *Die Musik in Geschichte und Gegenwart, Im Bärenreiter-Verlag Kassel und Basel*, 1952; Anna Steiniger, a Biographical Sketch, by John Storer Cobb, pub. G. Schirmer, Jr., Boston, Mass., 1886; "Editorial Bric-A-Brac," in Music, A monthly magazine, W. S. B. Mathews, Editor, pub. Chicago, Ill., September, 1900.

APPENDIX B. Musicians and Teachers Associated with Roës, who Applied the Teaching of Liszt

(Transposed from Chapter Two of *La Musique Mystère Réalité*)

For many years, Mme. Marie Stuart de Backer has followed very closely the new school, whose values she has grasped in a perfect manner, values such as Liszt shows us in his universal lesson. She applies his precepts with perspicacity and enthusiasm.

With Suzèlene van Hall, new conceptions following the old precepts of Weimar, are found full developed. Her ideas, applied with fervor, on the psychology of teaching, her new method on the theory of harmony, the consequences of harmonic analyses, her cult of the *Lied* put in practice in piano playing, give the most astonishing results. Her music sings through the most beautiful of executions.

Mme. Liénard, who teaches at the Russian Conservatory in Paris, has built her powerful playing on the principles of Liszt's school, and her many students do not fail to profit from her advice, which is of perfect clarity.

Some of the new adepts, like the excellent Dutch pianist Hendrik Poldermans, have studied extensively the principles of Weimar; they will not be long inculcating in their young pupils that which they themselves have acquired with conviction.

Let us not forget the professors who are forming new disciples in France. Among those who teach in the capital and its suburbs we wish to name the excellent painist Pierre Fiquet, Professor of the Conservatory of the tenth district of Paris, soloist Radio-Lausanne; and Professor Hubert Kurtzmann who transmits intelligently to his young pupils the rediscovered method.

In Belgium there is the young master Frédéric Gevers, well known through his many concert tours. The time will come when he will consecrate his activity to the profit of his students. And the prodigious talent of Louis Backx, Belgian also, . . . what will it bring? How heartening is the encouragement given to the young by the Belgian pianist and author, the master Emil Bosquet, former student and friend of Busoni!

In Finland, the master Timo Mikkilä imparts at Helsinki his profound experiences in the middle of a great circle of his compatriots for the most part remarkably gifted. We re-discover today in this country the imprint of the lessons given by Busoni at the Conservatory, now the Sibelius Academy.

In Switzerland, the astonishing Raffaele d'Allessandro, pianist, organist and composer of a considerable number of important works of a powerful and quite new musicianship, has arrived by degrees at the first

rank of musicians of our era. We also draw attention particularly to the enigmatic Maurice Perrin, pianist of multiple talent, professor at the Lausanne Conservatory.

In Italy, as we have said above, the memory of Busoni has excited in the hearts of his compatriots an enthusiasm for new ideas, the salient characteristic of this prodigious renovator.

In England, the school has continued under the impetus of Mme. Frieda van Dieren-Kindler, one of the favorite students of Busoni.

Egon Petri, one of the most eminent pianists of our times, also taught by the master of Florence,* pursues his activity in the United States. From time to time we hear some of his students, all equipped with a solid *métier* and surprising virtuosity.

These happy facts give us hope of a coming renaissance.

**Ed. note:* Roës and Petri were friends and fellow students of Busoni.

APPENDIX C. Works of Paul Roës

Musical works, unpublished. In 1957, the manuscripts were registered as "Posthumous" with the Society of Authors, Composers and Publishers of Music (S.A.C.E.M.).

Il Giorno (piano)	
Prelude for Piano	
Meditations on a Theme of Beethoven (piano)	(25 minutes)
La Vita Eterna (piano)	
Cadenza for Beethoven's Third Concerto	(20 minutes)
Lieder. Eight Melodies on texts of Baudelaire, Li-Tai-Po	
March for Piano	(4 minutes)
Second Concerto for Piano and Orchestra	(40 minutes)
Cycle du Jour, Five pieces for piano	
La Nuit, l'Aube, Midi, la 6e heure, le Crépuscule	(25 minutes)

Literary works, published by the firm of Henry Lemoine & Co. in Paris.

Essai sur la Technique du Piano - 1935
L'Élément Fondamental de la Technique, du Jeu chez Liszt et Chopin - 1937
La Musique et L'Artisan du Piano - 1939
La Technique Fulgurante de Busoni - 1941
La Musique Mystère et Réalité - 1955

Bibliography

Beethoven, Ludwig van. Letters to Bettina von Arnim.

Boissier, Mme. Auguste. Franz Liszt as Teacher, Paul Zsolnay, Verlag, Berlin.

Breithaupt, Rudolf M. *Die natürlich Klaviertechnik.* C. F. Kahnt Nachfolger, Leipzig. *Ed. note:* published in 3 parts (1905, 1909, 1919). Part 2 was translated into French, Russian and English.

Busoni, Ferruccio. Sketch for a New Aesthetic of the Art of Music (*Esquisse d'une nouvelle esthétique de l'art musical*), Insel-Verlag, Leipzig.

Carrel, Alexis. *Refléxions sur la conduite de la vie*, ed. Plon, Paris.

Chesterton, Gilbert Keith. The Writings of

Clarendon, Edward Hyde, Earl of. The Apotheosis of Verdi's Requiem. (article appearing in Figaro, May 2, 1953.)

Clark, Frederick Horace. *Liszt's Offenbahrung* (The Revelation of Liszt), ed. Viweg, Berlin, 1907.

Combarieu, Jules. History of Music, Vol. I, Armand Colin, Paris, 1953.

Cousinet, Roger. (reference to a short work of M. Cousinet on musical education, printed in *Les Presses d'Ile-de-France,* No. 15, March 1953, Paris.)

Diepenbrock, Alfons. In Memoriam (to Mahler).

Goethe, Johann Wolfgang. *Briefwechsel* (Correspondence).

Heine, Heinrich. The Writings of

Hello, Ernest. The Writings of

Houbraken, Arnold. Rembrandt van Rijn, La Haye, 1953.

Huysmans, J. K. En Route, Tresse & Stock, Paris, 1895.

Kant, Immanuel. The Writings of

Kleczynski, Jan. *Chopin's grössere Werke*, Leipzig, 1898.

Leibnitz, Gottfried Wilhelm. The Writings of

Liszt, Franz. Frédéric Chopin, Breitkopf and Härtel, Leipzig, 1923, 7th ed.

Masseron, Alexander. *La Divine Comédie*, French trans., Albin Michel, Paris, 1948-50.

Müller, Karl Otfried. *Geschichte der griechischen Literatur.* J. Max, Breslau, 1841. Also A. Heitz, Stuttgart, 1882-1884.

Nietzsche, Friedrich Wilhelm. Zarathustra.

Plato. The Banquet.

Ponceau, Amédée. *La musique et l'angoisse,* ed. *La Colombe*, Paris, 1951.

Pourtalès, Guy de. *La vie de Franz Liszt*, ed. Gallimard, Paris, 1927.

Rimbaud, J. Arthur. A Season in Hell, *Le Mercure de France*, Paris, 1914.

Roës, Paul. All published by Henry Lemoine & Co., Paris.
Essai sur la Technique du Piano—1935.
L'Élément Fondamental de la Technique, du Jeu chez Liszt et Chopin—1937.
La Musique et L'Artisan du Piano—1939.
La Technique Fulgurante de Busoni—1941.
La Musique Mystère et Réalité—1955.

Rolland, Romain. *Vie de Beethoven,* Hachette, 1922.

Valéry, Paul. The Writings of

Wessem, Constant van. Franz Liszt, pub. J.-P. Kruseman, The Hague, 1927.

Wieck, Clara. Journal.

Index of Names

Photo J. Roubier

Position of Roës at the piano

MUSIC, THE MYSTERY AND THE REALITY